FOREWORD ∞

The impact of historical coal mining on a landscape is rarely seen as clearly as at Cutacre, which, until recently, was an area dominated by a gigantic colliery spoil heap. Elsewhere much of the land has been removed by opencast mining. You could therefore be forgiven for thinking that not much of archaeological interest could possibly survive; however, archaeological investigations have revealed a remarkable range of sites from various periods stretching back to around 7000 years ago. Funded by UK Coal and the Harworth Group through a planning condition of consent to win the remaining coal and regenerate the site for commercial and other uses, this has been one of the largest archaeological landscape studies undertaken in Greater Manchester.

CONTE

It is important for archaeologists to let the local and wider community know about key discoveries from their investigations. At Cutacre, these discoveries were plentiful and include early prehistoric artefacts, a Middle Bronze Age settlement, medieval iron smelting, an early seventeenth-century great hall, as well as a farmstead of the same period. One of the remarkable aspects of the archaeological investigations has been the successful application of a variety of modern scientific techniques to maximise our understanding of the excavated evidence. All of this is described in this booklet in a well-illustrated and readable style, in common with the previous 23 volumes in the *Greater Manchester's Past Revealed* series. This booklet therefore represents an important aspect of the public benefit arising from the programme of archaeological work, and Oxford Archaeology North is to be congratulated on its production.

NORMAN REDHEAD,
Heritage Management Director,
Greater Manchester Archaeological Advisory Service

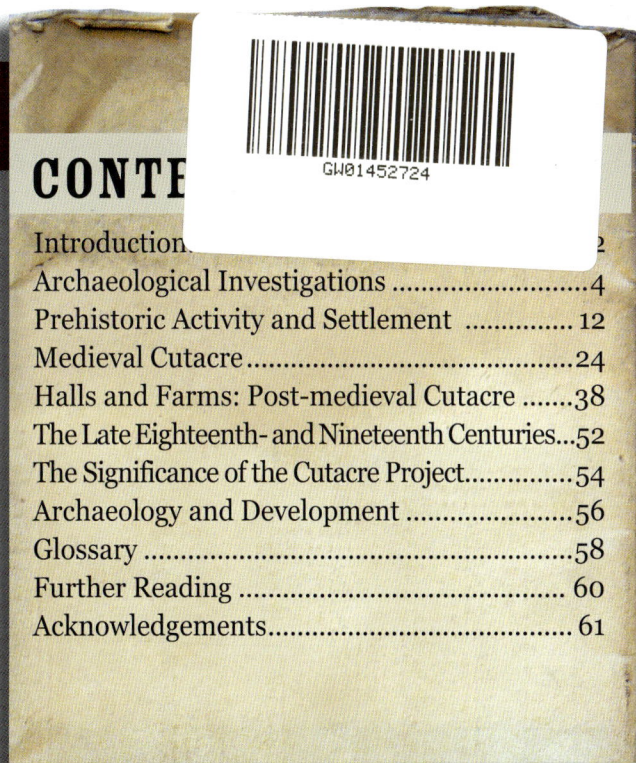

INTRODUCTION

Cutacre forms a 314ha (hectares) mixed-use commercial site and public open-space in Greater Manchester, some 4.75km to the south-east of Bolton. It straddles the three metropolitan boroughs of Bolton, Salford, and Wigan, and lies between the modern settlements of Little Hulton, in Walkden, Shakerley, in Atherton, and Over Hulton, in Westhoughton. Today, the site contains a mixture of woodland and wildlife areas, farmland, and also a commercial logistics area that opened in 2016.

A modern aerial view across Cutacre, looking east

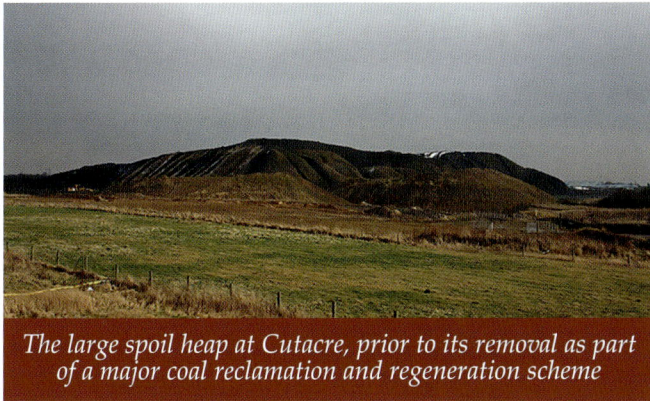

The large spoil heap at Cutacre, prior to its removal as part of a major coal reclamation and regeneration scheme

Immediately prior to the nineteenth century, Cutacre formed a rural landscape, typical of those on the Lancashire Coal Measures, in southern Lancashire. Hence, for much of its history, this landscape contained a smattering of farmsteads, some dating back to the prehistoric period, interspersed between agricultural fields and small areas of woodland. From at least the twelfth century AD onwards, up until the nineteenth century, there was also some small-scale rural industry within the area. Wharton Hall was also established during this period, creating a high-status dwelling.

Throughout the nineteenth century, the landscape of the Lancashire Coal Measures was transformed by large-scale industrial coal mining, which led, at Cutacre, to the creation of the largest spoil heap in Europe. This tip was in the eastern half of the development area, and had been partly created through mining activity associated with the former Charlton Colliery, the pit-head being adjacent to the north-western boundary of Cutacre, and also through the dumping of spoil, which had been transported from Brackley, Mosley Common, and Sandhole collieries. Another smaller coal tip was also constructed in the south-eastern part of Cutacre, which was associated with another former colliery, lying directly within the development area, known as Wharton Hall Colliery.

Between 2006 and 2011, these spoil heaps were reworked by UK Coal, which also undertook some surface mining, after which the area was restored and landscaped by the Harworth Group to create the present-day parkland and commercial area. During this period of reworking and restoration, an archaeological study was undertaken to identify any significant archaeological sites. This was then followed by targeted investigation that primarily aimed to record archaeological sites which might be affected by the reworking and redevelopment of the area. This booklet presents the results of this work, paying particular attention to the sites identified and recorded by an extensive campaign of archaeological excavation.

Archaeology is the study of past human activity through the identification, recording, and analysis of material remains. At Cutacre, a range of archaeological techniques was employed that were designed to identify and record any below-ground archaeological remains that might lie in this area.

Initially, the work consisted of several 'desk-based assessments' that considered the Cutacre area in some detail. In total, four of these studies were undertaken, which examined historical documents and pictures, maps, and aerial photographs. These studies also collated the information held in a database, termed the 'Historic Environment Record', which is maintained by the Greater Manchester local authorities. As part of the desk-based assessments, walkover surveys were also completed, which noted the presence of any visible archaeological features within the proposal area.

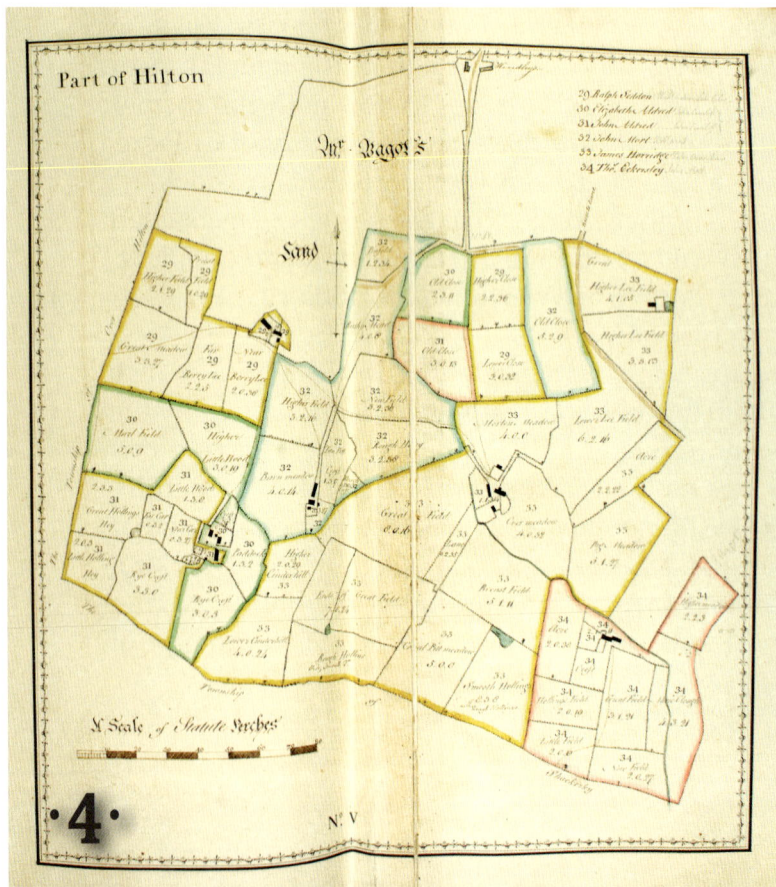

Importantly, the desk-based assessments identified 117 sites, which had varying levels of archaeological significance. These included post-medieval farmhouses, most of which had been demolished in the twentieth century, a high-status hall (Wharton Hall), also demolished in the twentieth century, together with ponds, coal-working and colliery sites, all of which were evident from historical maps. In addition, several potential small-scale medieval/post-medieval industrial sites were identified on the basis of historical field-name evidence (eg 'Kiln Meadow'; 'Cinder Hill').

An early map (c 1764) showing that part of Cutacre in the ownership of the Duke of Bridgewater (BW/E/1 Old Estate Plans reproduced courtesy of the Peel Archives and Salford City Archives)

Following the desk-based assessments, the plans for the reworking and reclamation of the site were considered, as to how these might affect potential archaeological sites and the upstanding historic buildings at Cutacre. An initial programme of work included a geophysical survey that aimed to locate and define any

Conducting the geophysical survey at Cutacre

buried remains that might be present at seven of the archaeological sites that had been identified from desk-based sources, relating to early coal mining and rural industry.

The processed magnetic data from the Cinder Hill site

0   100 m

1:2000

This survey comprised a detailed magnetic survey, utilising a gradiometer. This instrument can detect buried features, such as walls, pits, ditches, surfaces, and also furnaces, ovens, kilns, and metalwork, as these often have different magnetic properties from the natural geology. A survey grid was established across each of the sites and then gradiometer readings were taken at 0.25m intervals, along traverses spaced 1m apart.

Following the completion of these surveys, the collected magnetic data were downloaded into a computer package. This processed the data from each of the sites and produced a series of images, which allowed the form and positions of magnetic anomalies to be determined. It was apparent from these that most of the sites appeared to contain buried remains, which varied in significance and density.

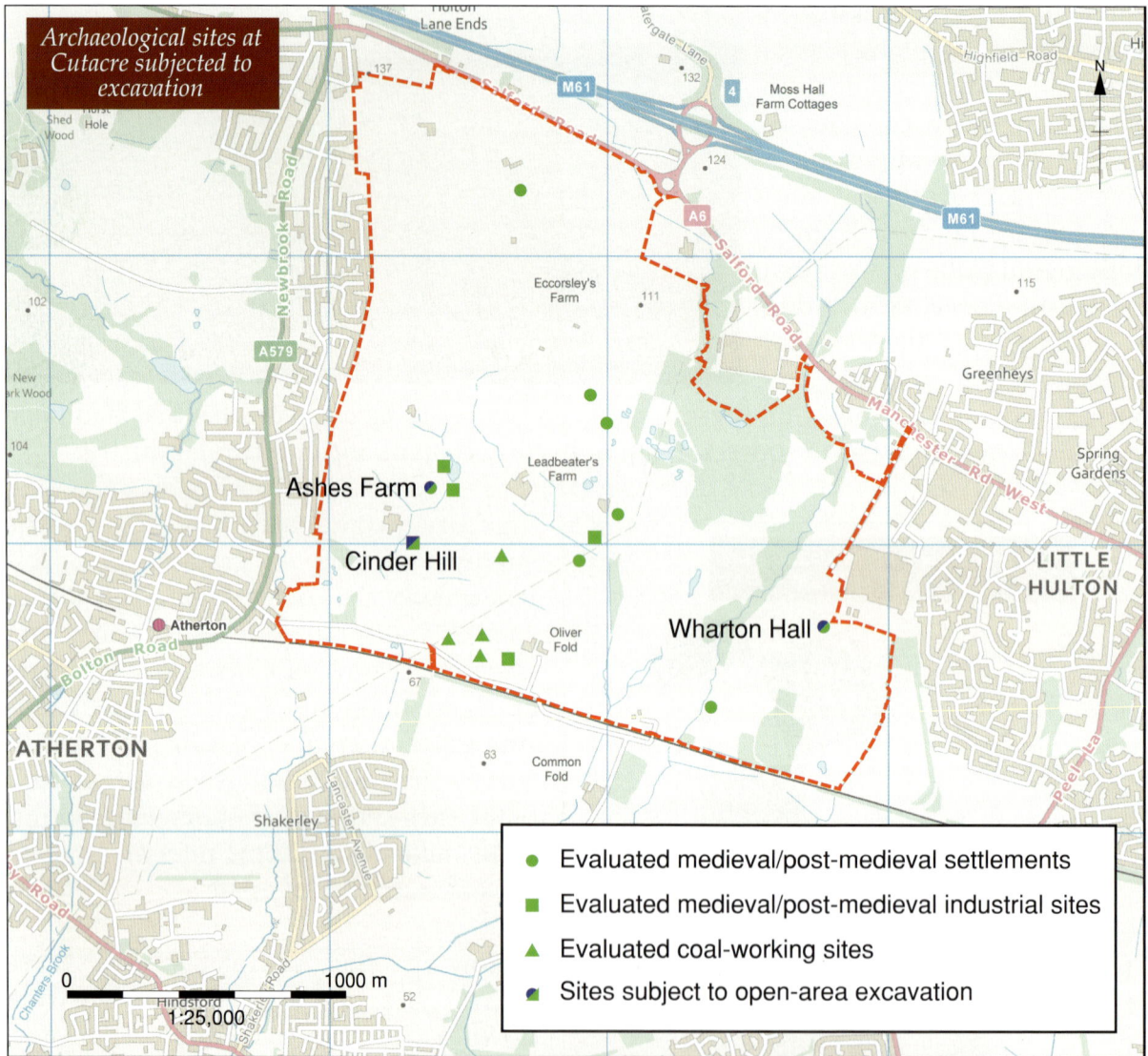

Archaeological sites at Cutacre subjected to excavation

Legend:
- ● Evaluated medieval/post-medieval settlements
- ■ Evaluated medieval/post-medieval industrial sites
- ▲ Evaluated coal-working sites
- Sites subject to open-area excavation

1:25,000

To enable the nature of the buried remains at the geophysical sites to be established, and also at the sites of several other potential medieval and post-medieval dwellings, the positions of which are depicted on eighteenth- and nineteenth-century maps, a scheme of archaeological trial trenching was then undertaken. This was designed to locate any significant archaeological remains that might be present, and determine their character, condition and date.

The scheme of trial trenching indicated that three of the targeted sites contained significant archaeological remains. These comprised structural remains associated with Ashes farm and Wharton Hall, two historic settlements, and dumps of metalworking slag at one of the industrial sites surveyed. Interestingly, these dumps lay within a field that was historically known as 'Cinder Hill', providing further evidence for early metalworking. Given the presence of these remains, an additional phase of large-scale archaeological excavation was completed between 2006 and 2008. This entailed excavating large

Archaeological trial trenching in progress

Mechanical stripping in progress during the large-scale excavation at Wharton Hall

·7·

open-area trenches, initially using a mechanical excavator and then by hand, to expose and record the complete extent of the buried remains at the respective sites.

At Ashes farm and Wharton Hall, this work comprised the excavation of single trenches, which at both sites exposed the footprints of post-medieval buildings, as well as associated structures and adjacent areas of cobbling and drainage. In addition, several 'negative' features, such as ditches, pits, and postholes, were present at both sites, together with artefacts, such as pottery.

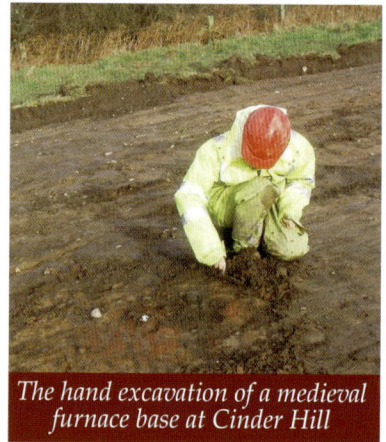

The hand excavation of a medieval furnace base at Cinder Hill

In contrast, the Cinder Hill site was divided into two areas, which would form the focus of separate excavations. Within the southern part of the site, two adjacent open-area trenches were excavated, which unexpectedly exposed prehistoric remains, in the form of 'negative' features and artefacts, whilst in the northern part of the site, a single trench was excavated, and this uncovered evidence for medieval iron production. These latter remains included furnace bases, associated structures and artefacts, as well as large volumes of metalworking waste (slag), which had clearly been responsible for the site being historically named 'Cinder Hill'.

Excavating Ashes farm

Following the completion of the archaeological fieldwork, the results from all phases of work were analysed by specialists. These included people with expertise in prehistoric, medieval and post-medieval artefacts, ancient plant remains, radiocarbon dating, and metalworking waste, as well as archaeological specialists who interpreted the structural remains uncovered by the excavations. These results were then synthesised and presented in a series of illustrated reports.

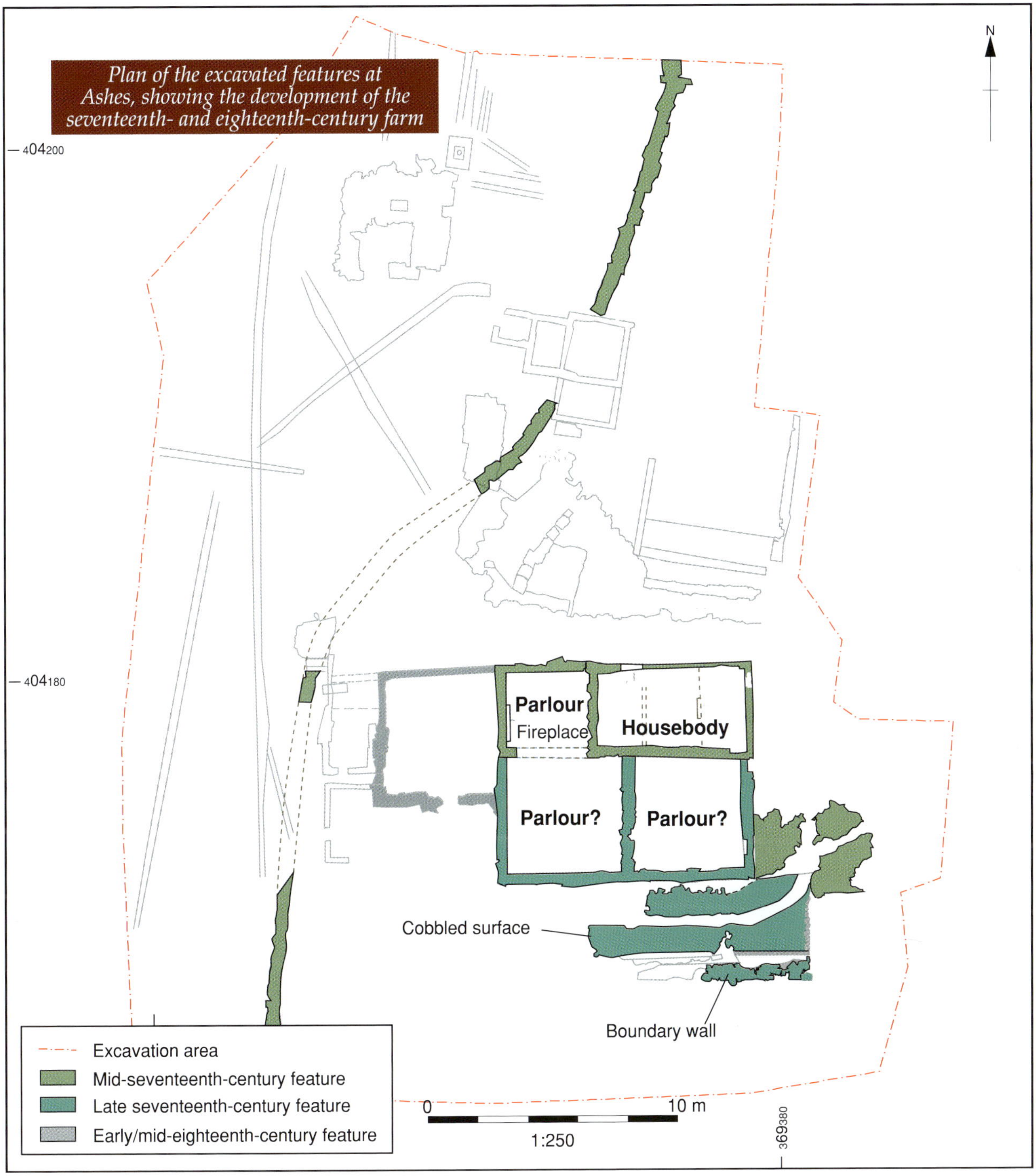

Plan of the excavated features at
Ashes, showing the development of the
seventeenth- and eighteenth-century farm

404200

404180

N

Parlour
Fireplace

Housebody

Parlour?

Parlour?

Cobbled surface

Boundary wall

Excavation area
Mid-seventeenth-century feature
Late seventeenth-century feature
Early/mid-eighteenth-century feature

0   10 m

1:250

369380

·9·

Ashes

Cinder Hill

*Modern aerial view of Cutacre locating the sites
subjected to open-area excavation*

Wharton Hall ⬤

PREHISTORIC ACTIVITY AND SETTLEMENT

The period prior to written records is called prehistory, and is subdivided into the Stone Age, Bronze Age, and Iron Age. The Stone Age is further subdivided into the Old Stone Age (Palaeolithic period) and Middle Stone Age (Mesolithic period), when a hunting-and-gathering lifestyle predominated, and the New Stone Age (Neolithic period), which witnessed the introduction of farming. The majority of prehistoric archaeology in the North West dates from the Mesolithic period onwards, from *c* 8000 cal BC until the mid-first century AD.

Significantly, the open-area excavations at Cinder Hill produced remains dating to the prehistoric period. This was particularly surprising, as at the start of the project it was considered that Cutacre only had a slight potential to contain evidence dating to this period. For instance, prior to the large-scale excavations, no prehistoric finds, such as stone tools or metalwork, had been recovered from the area, no obvious earthwork sites, marking the position of settlements or burials, were known, and the geophysical surveys and trial trenching had not detected any features that seemed prehistoric in date. It was also assumed that the surface geology of the Cutacre area, which comprises heavy, poorly drained deposits of glacial clay, was not particularly conducive to prehistoric settlement or agriculture. Indeed, large-scale excavation at Cinder Hill was undertaken to record the evidence for medieval iron production, detected by geophysical survey and trial trenching, and so the discovery of earlier archaeological remains at the site represented a major research bonus.

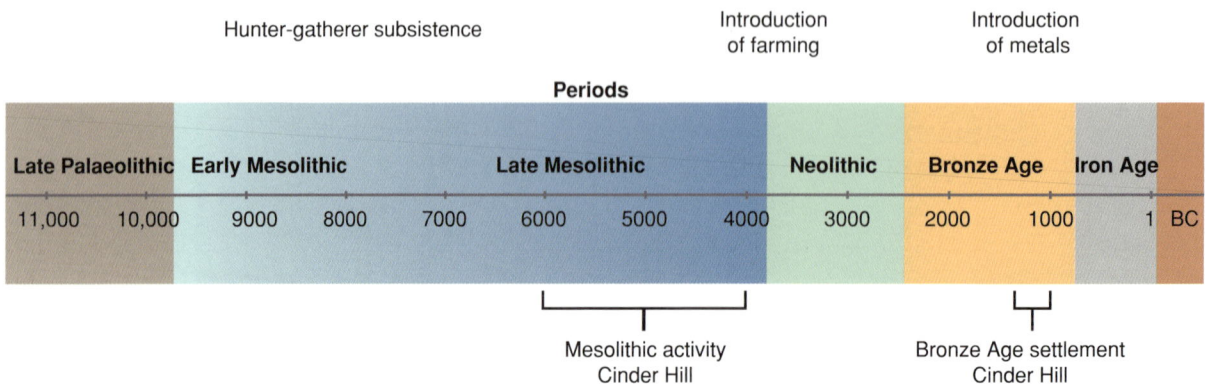

Hunter-gatherer subsistence				Introduction of farming	Introduction of metals	
Periods						
Late Palaeolithic	Early Mesolithic	Late Mesolithic		Neolithic	Bronze Age	Iron Age
11,000 10,000	9000 8000 7000	6000 5000 4000		3000	2000 1000	1 BC

Mesolithic activity
Cinder Hill

Bronze Age settlement
Cinder Hill

Mesolithic hunter-gatherers at Cutacre

The prehistoric remains at Cinder Hill date to two separate periods, with the earliest of these probably falling in the late Mesolithic period (*c* 6000-4000 cal BC), when small groups of hunter-gatherers were present in the Greater Manchester area. Archaeological investigations across the North West suggest that these Mesolithic groups were highly mobile, living in temporary structures, such as tents or bivouacs, and that they acquired all of their food and material from the natural environment. These groups visited and occupied different parts of the landscape on a seasonal basis. This was probably for economic reasons (for instance, following migratory routes of game and fish, acquiring specific woodland and other material resources available at certain times of the year), though it is also likely that certain places (such as mountains, caves, springs, islands and groves) may have been considered special, perhaps even sacred, and would have been the focus for religious practices. It also seems that, at certain times of year, some of the small

A 1773 engraving of a bivouac from a Haush encampment in Tierra del Fuego. The open-fronted structure seems comparable to the late Mesolithic structures excavated in north-west England

groups coalesced into larger gatherings, to take advantage of the more prolific seasonal resources that were found at specific locations (*eg* sites along rivers used to catch migratory fish). Such meetings would also allow these dispersed groups to meet, create alliances, exchange objects, and perhaps perform ceremonies and rites of passage.

Several palaeoenvironmental studies in Greater Manchester have analysed ancient plant remains as a way of reconstructing the historic environment. These studies imply that the landscape in which these late Mesolithic groups roamed was largely covered with deciduous woodland and scrub, inhabited by wolves, bears, beavers, roe and red deer, pigs and aurochs (giant wild cattle). However, the evidence also indicates that Mesolithic people intentionally created small openings and clearances within the primeval woodland, to allow game to browse, and perhaps to create small areas of coppice that could be revisited.

At Cutacre, the evidence for late Mesolithic people comprised a small collection of artefacts, consisting of worked flint and chert, and a larger basalt pebble that had been used as a hammer or grinding stone. The flint and chert was probably obtained locally, as pebbles in these materials are found in the geology of the area, which could have been acquired by searching the beds or banks of rivers.

Several different types of worked-stone tools were present that could have been used for cutting and scraping, along with two very characteristic Mesolithic tool types, known as microliths. These are small pieces of worked stone, chipped from blades that had been struck off a core, and, as with those from Cutacre, they normally have geometric or crescent forms. Once the microliths had been produced, it was normal to haft several together to make a composite tool. These might have been spears or arrows, or could have been used for carving wood and bone, for hide-working, or for processing plant materials.

Importantly, the Mesolithic artefacts from Cinder Hill only consisted of complete, usable tools, and this seems to indicate that artefacts were not made at the site. This, in turn, suggests that this area was only briefly visited by late Mesolithic people. Although the precise reason for their presence is unclear, it may be significant that some of the tools were recovered from tree-throws. The association of Mesolithic artefacts with these features may suggest that the intentional felling or uprooting of trees was one early activity occurring at the site. This perhaps created a small woodland clearance, and hence

the tree-throws and tools are rare and direct evidence for a small Mesolithic clearance, such as those detected in the palaeoenvironmental records for the region. However, another possibility is that the trees were naturally uprooted and then acted as markers/foci for early activity. Indeed, it has been noted that many excavated Mesolithic-period tree-throws across England also contain stone tools. This may therefore suggest that naturally created 'pits', such as those at Cinder Hill, were in some way 'special' for Mesolithic people, who accordingly placed small offerings within them.

Another feature that might possibly have been associated with Mesolithic people visiting the site was a small pit, that was filled with fire-cracked stones. This was found within the area covered by tree-throws and one possibility is that it represents the remains of a hearth or cooking pit.

The possible early prehistoric hearth or cooking pit

A Bronze Age settlement at Cinder Hill

In addition to the Mesolithic tools, important remains relating to a later prehistoric settlement were also uncovered during the large-scale excavation at Cinder Hill. This lay on the downslope of the hill and appears to have been placed at the confluence of two watercourses. Hence, access to water may have been an important consideration for those who established this settlement. One of these watercourses flowed to the east of the settlement and was defined by a present-day stream, whilst the other was to the west, being a silted-up river channel (a palaeochannel), which was only visible in the excavation trench.

The date that the settlement was occupied was determined through scientific dating. It contained several contemporary components, which produced charred plant remains and wood charcoal that were eminently suitable for radiocarbon dating. Seven samples were submitted for dating and when the results are considered together these indicate that the settlement dates to the latter half of the second millennium BC, being occupied at some point between 1480 cal BC and 1080 cal BC, during a period classified as the Middle Bronze Age. Based on this date, there is a gap, therefore, of up to 4500 years, between the late Mesolithic visit to Cinder Hill, and the establishment of the Bronze Age settlement. During this time, which covers the Neolithic period and Early Bronze Age, there is no evidence for any prehistoric activity at Cutacre, though small communities of farmers were certainly active in the wider region.

The roundhouse

The Middle Bronze Age settlement at Cinder Hill contained a single roundhouse. This had a diameter of *c* 7m which, given its relatively small size, probably housed a single family. Architecturally, its superstructure was composed of a ring of oak and ash posts, which supported the roof, as well as acting as the outer wall of the house. These posts were widely spaced and the gaps between may have been filled

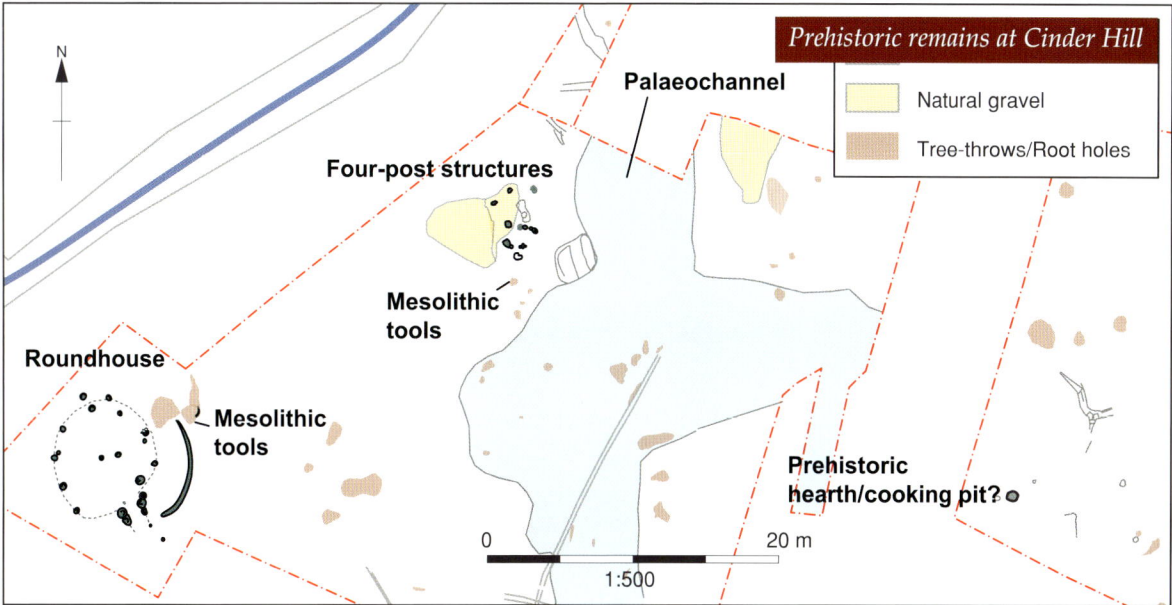

Prehistoric remains at Cinder Hill

Natural gravel

Tree-throws/Root holes

Palaeochannel

Four-post structures

Mesolithic tools

Roundhouse

Mesolithic tools

Prehistoric hearth/cooking pit?

0   20 m

1:500

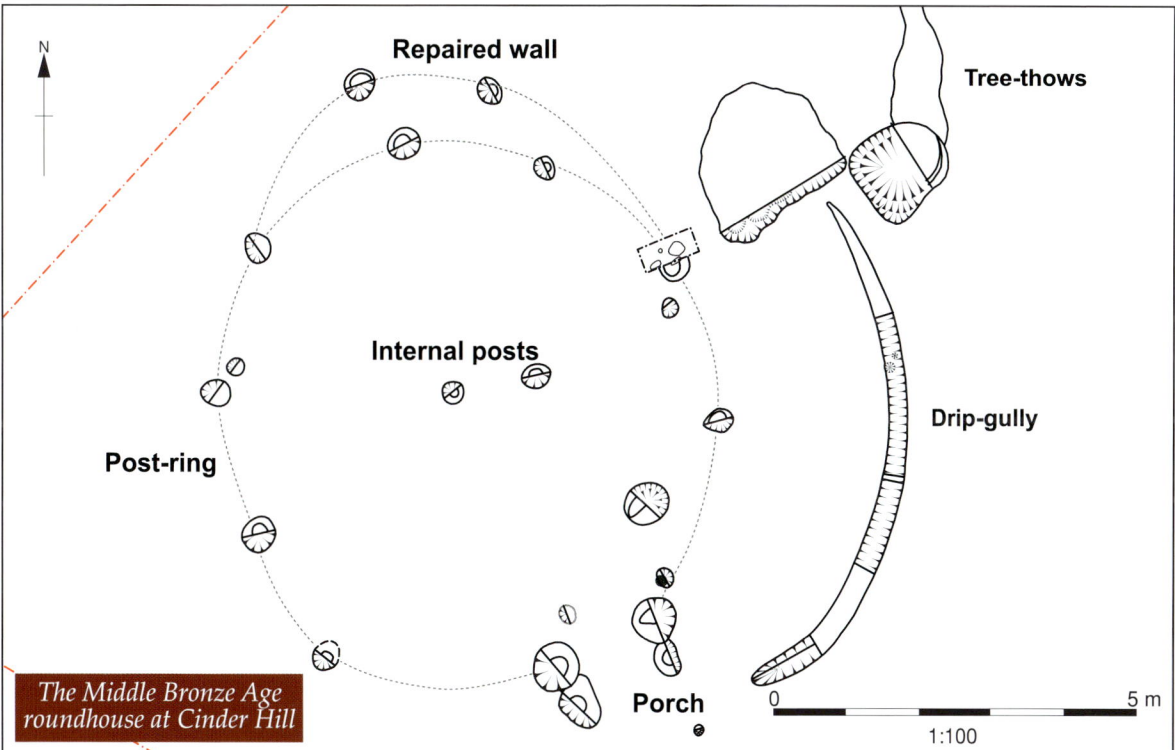

Repaired wall

Tree-thows

Internal posts

Drip-gully

Post-ring

Porch

0   5 m

1:100

The Middle Bronze Age roundhouse at Cinder Hill

·**17**·

Part of the Bronze Age roundhouse at Cinder Hill, following stripping of the site, the drip-gully being visible as a dark arc, whilst the postholes are defined by circular patches of dark soil

by wattle and daub, or perhaps prefabricated panels. Two posts were also present in the interior, one of which stood at the dead centre; however, it is likely that these were not load-bearing elements of the roundhouse *per se*, but were instead present as supports only during its initial construction.

The entrance to the house was defined by a projecting porch, aligned to the south-east. Such porches were a common feature of later prehistoric roundhouses, and appear to have been used both to shelter and embellish the entranceway. Similarly, south-easterly aligned entrances were also common in later prehistoric roundhouses. The precise reasons for this choice of orientation are unknown, though it has been argued that this may have related to the rising sun, particularly at the equinoxes and the mid-winter solstice. However, at a practical level, a doorway to the south-east would provide shelter from the prevailing south-westerly wind and maximise the amount of daylight entering the dwelling. The Cinder Hill roundhouse also had a drip-gully, which collected rainwater from its roof. Its position indicates that the eaves of the structure overhung the outer wall line by some 2m.

The Bronze Age roundhouse at Cinder Hill following the excavation of its postholes. The upright timbers mark their positions, with the porch on the right

Ancillary structures

Apart from the roundhouse, the settlement also contained two four-post structures, positioned 31m to the north-east of the roundhouse, next to the palaeochannel. The earlier of these, c 1 x 1.65m in plan, had been destroyed by fire, after which it was replaced by the second structure, which was near identical in size and layout. These were also shielded by a fence that probably acted as a windbreak.

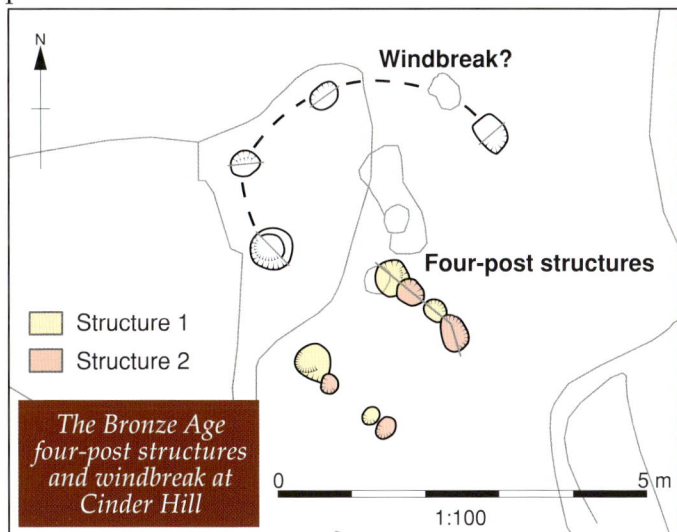

The Bronze Age four-post structures and windbreak at Cinder Hill

Nationally, four-post structures are common features of later prehistoric settlements. They are often interpreted as granaries, with a floor raised above ground level, protecting the stored grain from damp and also vermin.

A reconstructed later prehistoric raised structure (interpreted as a granary; foreground) and roundhouse (background) at Castell Henllys, Pembrokeshire, Wales. The reconstructions are based on excavated evidence, the forms being comparable to the Bronze Age structures at Cinder Hill (© Crown copyright: Royal Commission on the Ancient and Historical Monuments of Wales)

At Cinder Hill, a large collection of burnt cereals was found in the postholes of these structures. This provided a valuable insight into their function and also the crops that were grown in the surrounding area.

These cereals had probably been charred when the earlier structure had burnt down, and mainly comprised barley, including naked barley and a many-rowed (probably six-row) variety. Several wheat grains were also present, and although it was not possible to identify these to type, based on the evidence from other Bronze Age settlements in the North West, they were probably emmer wheat. Given the 'standard' interpretation of four-post structures as granaries, one possibility is that these cereals represent foodstuff that was stored within the primary structure, prior to it being burnt down. However, in damp climates, it was normal to store cereals in a semi-processed

state, as a means of protecting the grain, and there was no clear evidence for this. Indeed, the analysed samples appeared to represent a fully processed crop, rather than grain that was going to be stored.

So, if, as it seems, the four-post structures at Cinder Hill did not act as granaries, can an alternative function be suggested? With this in mind, one distinct feature of the cereal assemblage was that numerous sprouted, or part-sprouted, barley grains were present, indicating that the cereals had germinated. Whilst this might suggest that they represent a spoilt harvest, another possibility is that they were the remains of intentionally malted grain. There is a significant amount of evidence to suggest that the malting of cereal grains was widely practised in prehistoric Britain and malted grain would have acted as an excellent source of B-vitamins; it is also the prime ingredient for sweet malt (an ingredient for barley cakes and malt porridge), and for brewing ale.

The intercutting postholes defining the north-eastern side of the two sequential four-post structures, filled with burnt material from the destruction of the earlier structure

Based on the processes used in traditional malting (as documented in the nineteenth century), this would first have involved soaking the grain in a vessel to increase its bulk by 25%. Water for this process could, therefore, have been obtained from the nearby palaeochannel, which may then have contained an active stream, or held standing water. The next step in the process involved

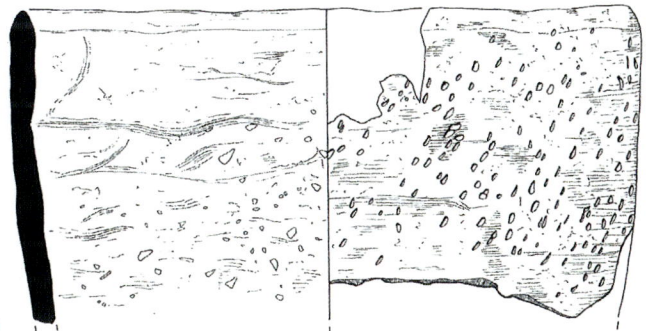

Middle Bronze Age pottery vessel

draining the grain and piling it into another vessel, for two to three days, where it began to germinate. Interestingly, fragments of Bronze Age pottery were recovered from the postholes of the four-post structures, derived from barrel-shaped jars. It is therefore possible that these were used both to soak and germinate the grain.

In the traditional malting process, after germination had commenced, the grain was spread out on a malting floor. It therefore seems possible that the four-post structures at Cinder Hill actually supported raised malting floors and functioned as prehistoric malting houses. If this was the case, the germinated grain on these raised floors would have been turned at intervals, over a two-week period, to achieve an even growth. Once this had occurred, the grains would be 'parched' over a hearth, or in an oven or kiln, to halt the germination process. Although at Cinder Hill no remains of any hearth or oven, which could have parched the malted grain, were identified, it is possible that such activities may have occurred between the four-post structures and the windbreak. Indeed, this would also explain the requirement for a windbreak in this part of the settlement, and an accident involving this hearth/oven might even explain how the first four-post structure was burnt down.

The Cutacre settlement in context

Archaeological evidence from the North West suggests that during the Middle Bronze Age the area was home to a scattering of small communities which practised small-scale mixed farming, within areas of clearance, living in open settlements that rarely contained more than three houses. Given this, the Cinder Hill settlement appears to be typical of the Middle Bronze Age in the region.

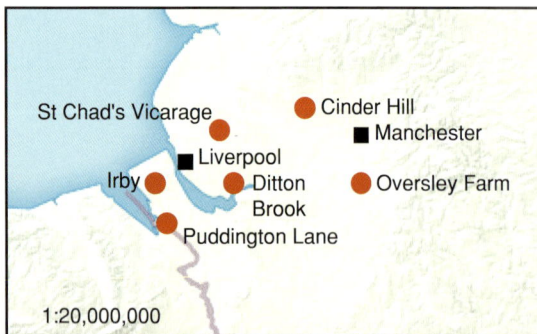

Middle Bronze Age sites in the Mersey Basin

However, it is worth noting that Bronze Age settlement remains in Greater Manchester, and the Mersey Basin more generally, are extremely rare. In fact, the features at Cinder Hill represent the first definitive example of a Bronze Age settlement examined in Greater Manchester, whilst the roundhouse is the earliest dated house within the metropolitan county!

Beyond Greater Manchester, the Cinder Hill settlement also represents only the second definitive Middle Bronze Age settlement (*ie* that associated with a house) to have been identified within the Mersey Basin, with the other being at Irby on the Wirral peninsula. At that site, a scattering of postholes may define either one large roundhouse, or three slightly smaller houses, which included two consecutive houses built on the same spot. In both scenarios, however, the houses have unusually large diameters, and it has therefore been suggested that these might actually have formed communal buildings, serving several family groups, as opposed to a single-family domestic dwelling, such as that at Cinder Hill.

The only other Middle Bronze Age sites from the Mersey Basin include a hearth from Puddington Lane, and isolated pits at Oversley Farm, Cheshire, now covered by Manchester Airport's second runway, and Ditton Brook, Merseyside. Another site that has produced Middle Bronze Age remains is St Chad's Vicarage, Kirby. There, two slightly arcing gullies were excavated that it has been argued formed elements of structures, probably securing windbreaks.

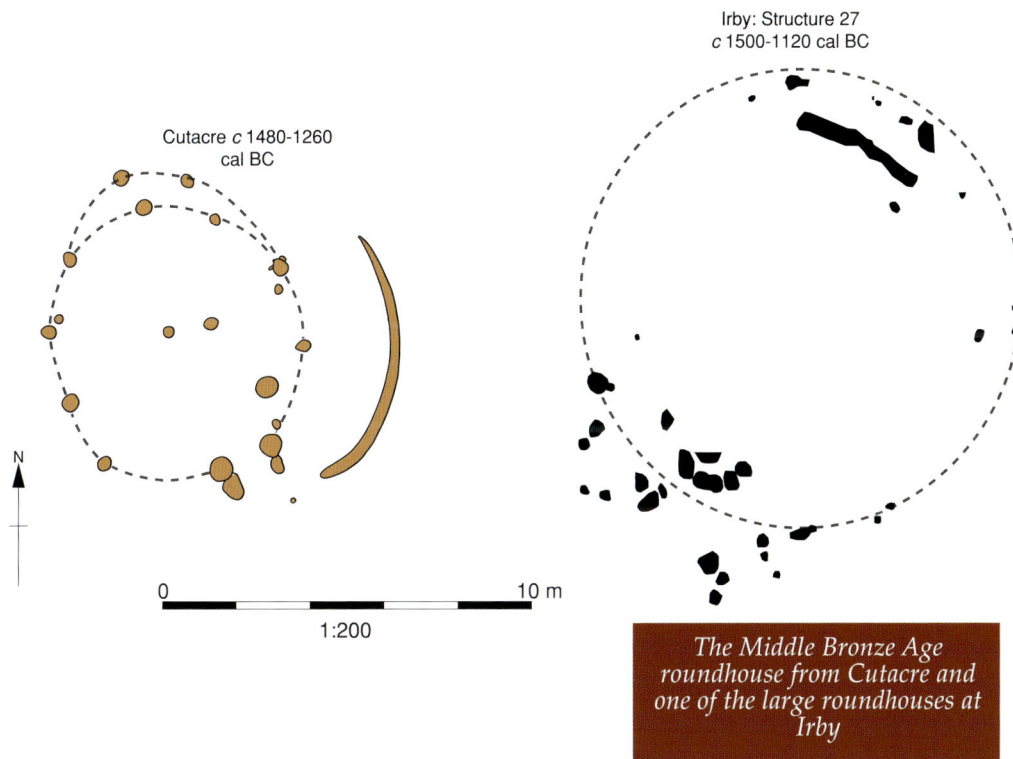

Irby: Structure 27
c 1500-1120 cal BC

Cutacre *c* 1480-1260 cal BC

N

0   10 m

1:200

The Middle Bronze Age roundhouse from Cutacre and one of the large roundhouses at Irby

·23·

With the demise of the Bronze Age settlement at Cinder Hill, definitive evidence for activity through the remainder of the prehistoric period (first millennium BC), and also the Roman period (late first century to mid-fifth century AD), is absent at Cutacre, as no remains dating to these periods were uncovered by the archaeological investigations. In fact, it is not until the medieval period that evidence for activity in this area is found.

This period covers approximately 1000 years, beginning with the end of Roman rule in Britain in the mid-fifth century AD, and continuing up until the 1540s. It tends to be divided into two separate eras, with the Norman Conquest of 1066 forming a watershed. The earlier of these, the early medieval period, or the Dark Ages, initially witnessed the formation of several small British kingdoms, but from the mid-seventh century onwards it was dominated by Anglo-Saxon kingdoms, with Cutacre lying within the kingdom of Northumbria. The ninth and tenth centuries were a time when the country was invaded by Viking armies, which caused the collapse of many of the Anglo-Saxon kingdoms, though the Vikings then effectively integrated with the local populations. The expansion of Wessex began at the end of the ninth century, which ultimately created England. Archaeological evidence from across the North West indicates that rural settlement during this period often comprised one or more timber (in the lowlands) or, in the uplands, stone rectangular buildings, which were sometimes associated with small enclosures, and sometimes also a very characteristic type of sunken-floored building.

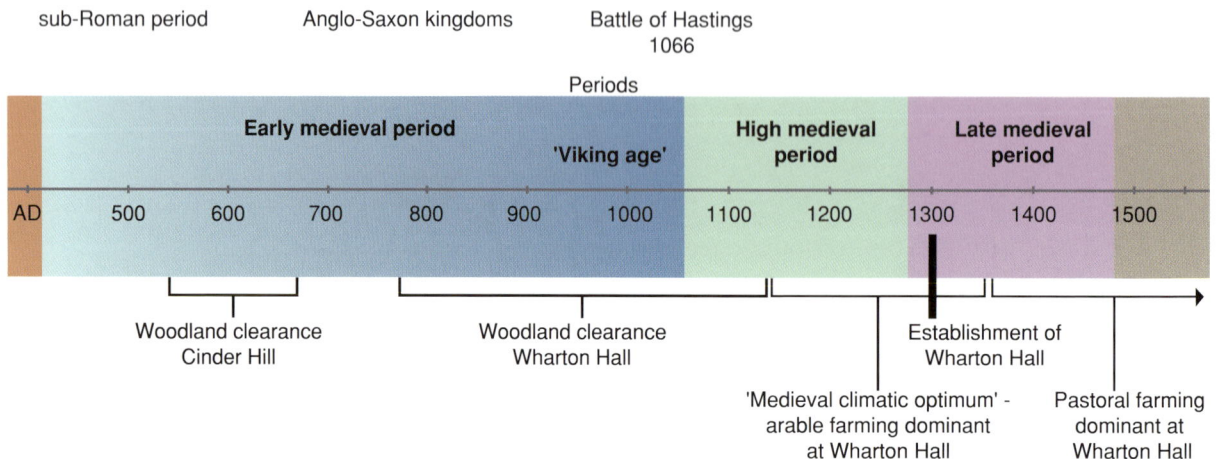

sub-Roman period	Anglo-Saxon kingdoms	Battle of Hastings 1066			

Periods

Early medieval period		'Viking age'	High medieval period	Late medieval period	

AD	500	600	700	800	900	1000	1100	1200	1300	1400	1500

Woodland clearance Cinder Hill

Woodland clearance Wharton Hall

Establishment of Wharton Hall

'Medieval climatic optimum' - arable farming dominant at Wharton Hall

Pastoral farming dominant at Wharton Hall

The late medieval period is defined initially by the imposition of Norman rule across the country. In the 500 years that are defined as this, in *c* 1150-1350, a warm climate existed (referred to as the 'medieval climatic optimum') that seems to have allowed agriculture to expand, which in turn led to a surge in population. However, this changed in the mid-fourteenth century, which is characterised by a climatic downturn, famine and plague, and the country was only just recovering from this, and the civil wars of the fifteenth century (known today as the Wars of the Roses), by the end of the reign of Henry VIII. Rural settlement throughout the late medieval period was characterised by small farmsteads and also larger medieval halls, which were the homes of the land-owning class.

The Anglo-Saxon landscape

Prior to the archaeological investigation, there was a clear suggestion that Cutacre contained some areas of Anglo-Saxon settlement, the place-names ascribed to the three units of land, known as townships, in the Cutacre area being Old English in origin. These were Tyldesley cum Shakerley, in the southern part of Cutacre, and Little Hulton and Middle Hulton, covering its northern part.

Tyldesley and Shakerley contain the element -ley, derived from the Old English *leah*, meaning a 'woodland' or 'clearing in a wood', and these probably denote the presence of a settlement within a wooded environment. In contrast, Little Hulton, Middle Hulton, and also the township of Over Hulton, immediately west of Cutacre, share a name, originally Hilton, which probably referred to the same location, namely a farmstead/estate (*tun*) on a hill (*hyll*). Given these names, it is also feasible that one or more of these townships existed as defined units of land in the early medieval period. Indeed, many townships in the North West appear to have Anglo-Saxon origins, forming a small unit of land within a larger manor, which was itself situated within a larger administrative block known as a hundred.

Although during the archaeological investigation no direct evidence, in the form of houses or enclosures, was discovered relating to these suspected Anglo-Saxon settlements, early medieval plant remains were recovered from the Cinder Hill and Wharton Hall excavations that suggested the presence of nearby settlement. At Cinder Hill, in Middle Hulton township, these included a small fragment of alder charcoal. This was radiocarbon dated to cal AD 540-660 and may have been produced during the burning of woodland to create a clearing for a settlement or agricultural plot.

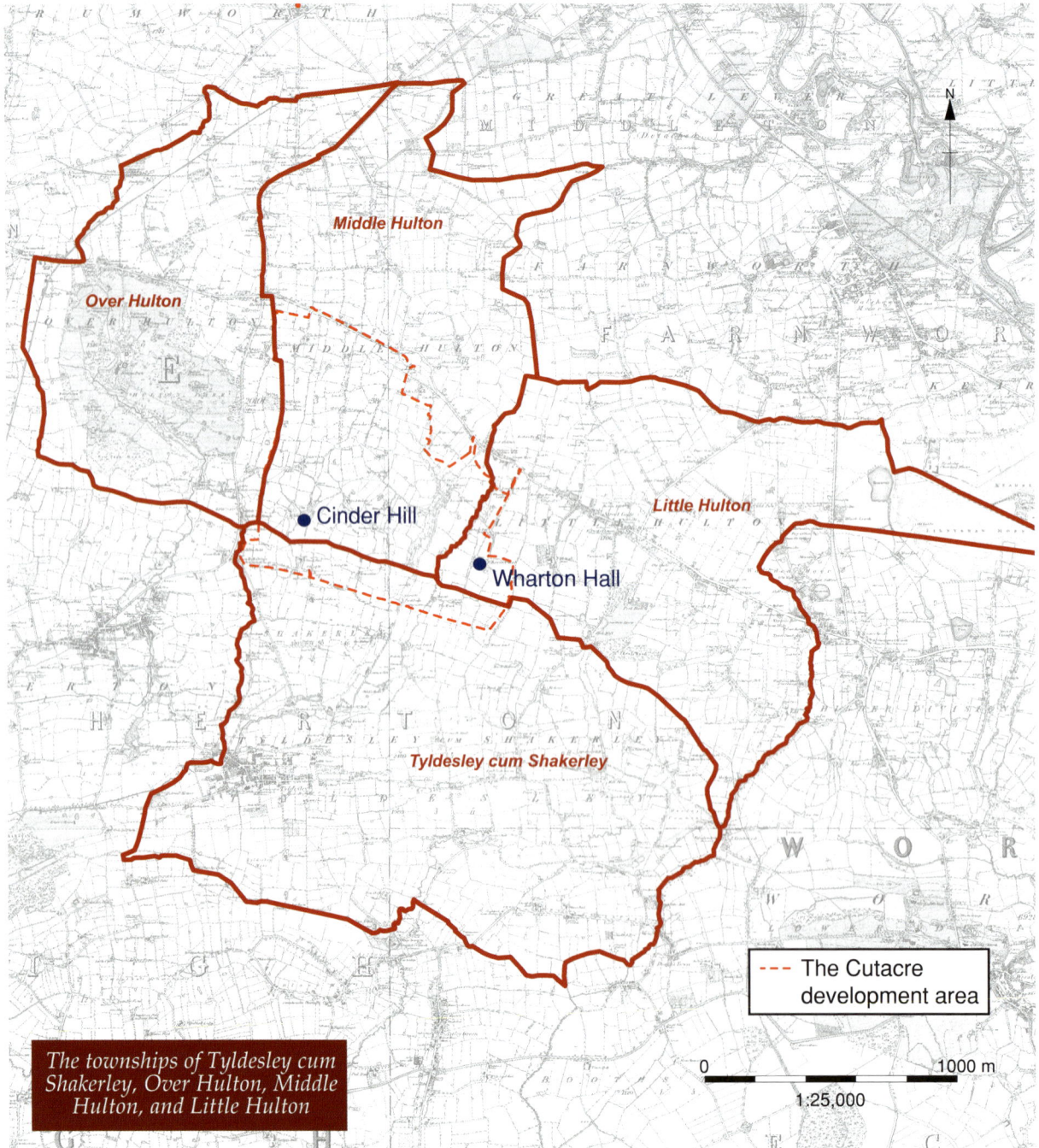

Middle Hulton

Over Hulton

Cinder Hill

Wharton Hall

Little Hulton

Tyldesley cum Shakerley

The townships of Tyldesley cum Shakerley, Over Hulton, Middle Hulton, and Little Hulton

The Cutacre development area

0   1000 m

1:25,000

·26·

More evidence for the medieval environment was present at Wharton Hall, where a palaeochannel was identified, which had gradually filled in the medieval period. It was evident that the sediments found at the top of the channel dated to the late medieval period, whilst those closer to the bottom were early medieval in date. Pollen, from plants in the wider landscape, had become incorporated into these sediments, and it was possible to record and count the different species of plants that were present in a core taken through them. This allowed the environment at different points in the medieval period to be established, which were then depicted on a pollen diagram.

This pollen diagram indicates that, although much of the early medieval landscape was wooded, both cereal cultivation and pastoral farming did occur close to Wharton Hall, within clearances. Numerous minute fragments of charcoal were also recorded in the early medieval sediments. These fragments derived from nearby burning, that was perhaps associated with woodland clearance or even a settlement. Together, the charcoal and pollen evidence indicate that an early medieval settlement must once have existed somewhere comparatively close to Wharton Hall. Indeed, as Wharton Hall was within Little Hulton township, it is possible that this settlement is that 'farmstead/estate', which is referenced by the *tun* element within the place-name Hulton.

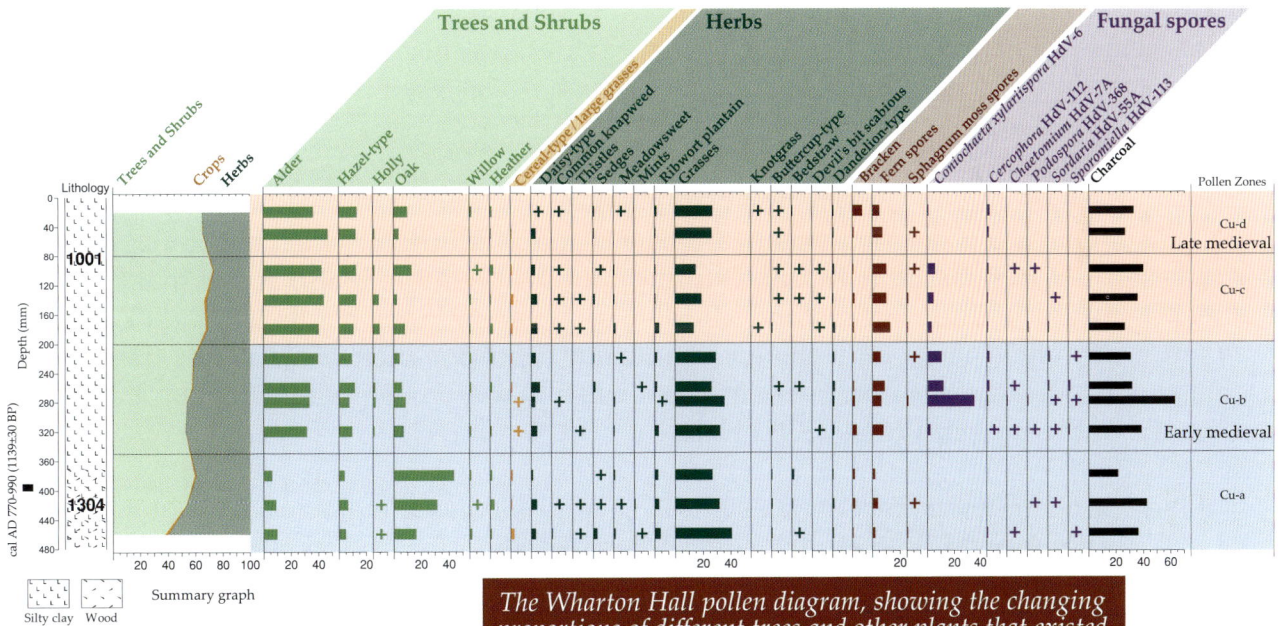

The Wharton Hall pollen diagram, showing the changing proportions of different trees and other plants that existed within the palaeochannel sediments

·27·

Late medieval Cutacre

Landscape and settlement

The pollen from the palaeochannel at Wharton Hall also provides insights into the late medieval landscape at Cutacre. From this, it is clear that arable farming predominated between the mid-twelfth and mid-fourteenth centuries, which appears to relate to the warmer climate that existed during this period (the 'medieval climatic optimum'). However, this pattern was reversed from the mid-fourteenth century onwards, when cereal cultivation dramatically decreased, with the landscape seemingly given over to pastoral farming.

Additional details relating to the late medieval landscape at Cutacre and its immediate environs were uncovered by historical research forming part of the archaeological investigation. This indicated that in the early thirteenth century the southern part of Cutacre (covered by Tyldesley cum Shakerley township) was held by the de Tyldesleys, who took their name from the township. However, in 1301, Henry de Tyldesley divided this area between his two sons and thus effectively created two manors within the same township. Each of these manors contained separate high-status halls, known as the Garrett and Cleworth Hall, though these were beyond the Cutacre development area. It is also evident that another late medieval unit of land, forming the hamlet of Shakerley, was created in the north-west part of the township, also partly within Cutacre. Although this hamlet was initially owned by the de Tyldesleys, in the early thirteenth century it was given to Cockersand Abbey, under which it was then held by the de Shakerley family, living at Shakerley Hall.

In the northern part of Cutacre, the documentary evidence indicates that, following the Norman Conquest, the area was within the manor of Hulton, which encompassed the townships of Little Hulton, Middle Hulton, and Over Hulton. It also seems that by 1212 the townships of Little Hulton and Middle Hulton were in the hands of the de Worsley family, who held these until the early fifteenth century, when their estates passed by marriage to the de Masseys. These families had a manor house in Worsley, probably on the site of the present Worsley Old Hall.

The documentary evidence indicates that several medieval halls and farms existed in Little Hulton and Middle Hulton townships. In Middle Hulton, these included Wood Hall, documented in 1354, and Edge Hall, documented in the early fifteenth century. The precise location of both of these halls is unknown, though land forming part of the Wood

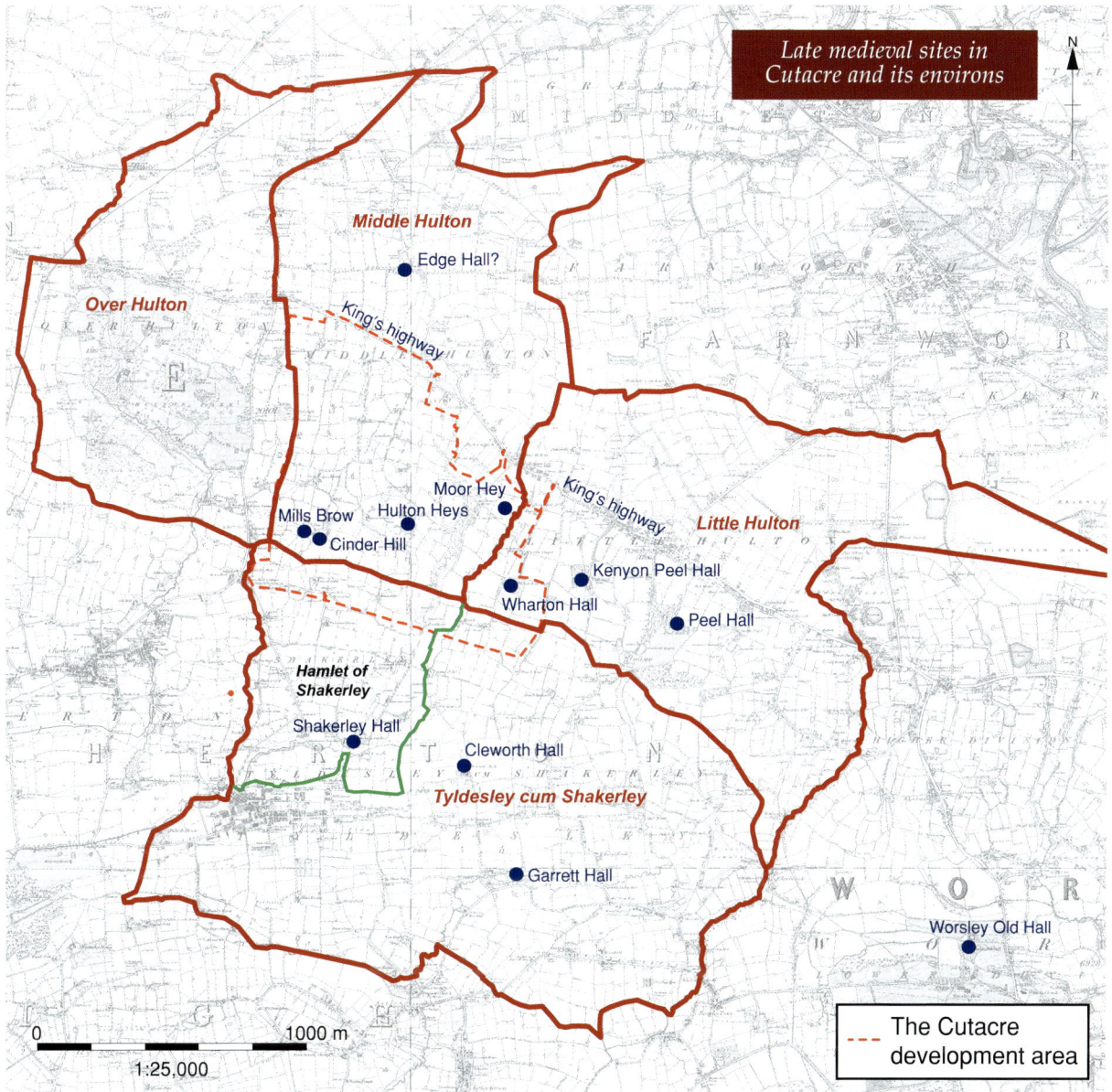

Over Hulton

Middle Hulton

Edge Hall?

King's highway

Mills Brow

Hulton Heys

Cinder Hill

Moor Hey

King's highway

Little Hulton

Kenyon Peel Hall

Wharton Hall

Peel Hall

Hamlet of
Shakerley

Shakerley Hall

Cleworth Hall

Tyldesley cum Shakerley

Garrett Hall

Worsley Old Hall

0   1000 m

1:25,000

The Cutacre
development area

Hall estate probably lay at Moor Hey, on the eastern edge of Cutacre, whilst Edge Hall
may have been at the site of a later farm known as Edge Fold, to the north of Cutacre. It
is also possible that this hall was originally a manor house that was occupied by the de
Worsley family. A survey of the area dating to the early fifteenth century also indicates

that there were six farm tenements in Middle Hulton at this time. The locations of these farms are not specified, but one was probably in the Cutacre area, at Hulton Heys. This site was accordingly subjected to archaeological evaluation, but no medieval remains were identified.

A potential medieval hall was also at Wharton Hall, in Little Hulton, in the south-eastern corner of Cutacre, based on the documentary evidence. At this site, the first explicit mention of a hall dates from 1582, and hence to the beginning of the post-medieval period, when it was in the ownership of William Warton. However, there is also a succession of references to the de Warton, or de Waverton, family as local landowners in Little Hulton throughout the medieval period, with the earliest reference to their estate dating to 1295. Given this, it is highly likely that Wharton Hall actually dates back to that time.

Based on the possible existence of the de Warton's medieval hall, during the excavation, one of the main aims was to identify any medieval structural remains, such as walls and floors, that might be related to this building. Although a fairly extensive area was excavated, no such remains were encountered, which could be equated either with a medieval hall, or other early buildings. However, a small collection of medieval objects was recovered, including fragments of medieval pottery and 14 pieces of medieval window glass. This derives from a leaded window, the design preserved on one fragment suggesting a simple grisaille pattern; significantly, glass of this period is only found in high-status or ecclesiastical buildings. This technique was popular in the thirteenth to fifteenth centuries, and it is therefore highly likely that it came from a window in the suspected medieval hall, or from an ancillary family chapel. Based on this evidence, it is likely that the structural remains associated with a medieval hall were comprehensively destroyed in the early post-medieval period, during the construction of a 'new' hall, the remains of which were clearly visible in the excavation area.

Degraded fragments of medieval window glass from Wharton Hall

Medieval iron production

At Cutacre, undoubtedly the best evidence for late medieval activity came from Cinder Hill, in Middle Hulton township. At an early stage of the project, it was suspected that the place-name 'Cinder Hill' might denote the site of kilns or furnaces, which had produced large quantities of industrial waste, in the form of slag ('cinder'). The presence of this waste was confirmed by the magnetic survey of the site, and also during trial trenching. Based on these results, large-scale excavation was undertaken which resulted in the important discovery of a late medieval bloomery, where iron ore was converted (smelted) into wrought iron, that could then be used to make iron tools and other implements.

Bloomeries were small sites that were used seasonally, and they were normally close to a water source, used for washing the ore, puddling clay, and quenching. They were also usually adjacent to an area of woodland, which provided the fuel, in the form of charcoal, required for smelting. Indeed, obtaining charcoal was key to iron production, as several tons needed to be burnt for every ton of iron ore smelted. The iron ore might have been either directly extracted from the local geology, or in some areas could be obtained from bogs (as bog iron), where percolating iron-bearing groundwater had oxidised to form accumulations of impure iron. Once recovered, the iron ore was also normally roasted, to make it more suitable for the smelting process.

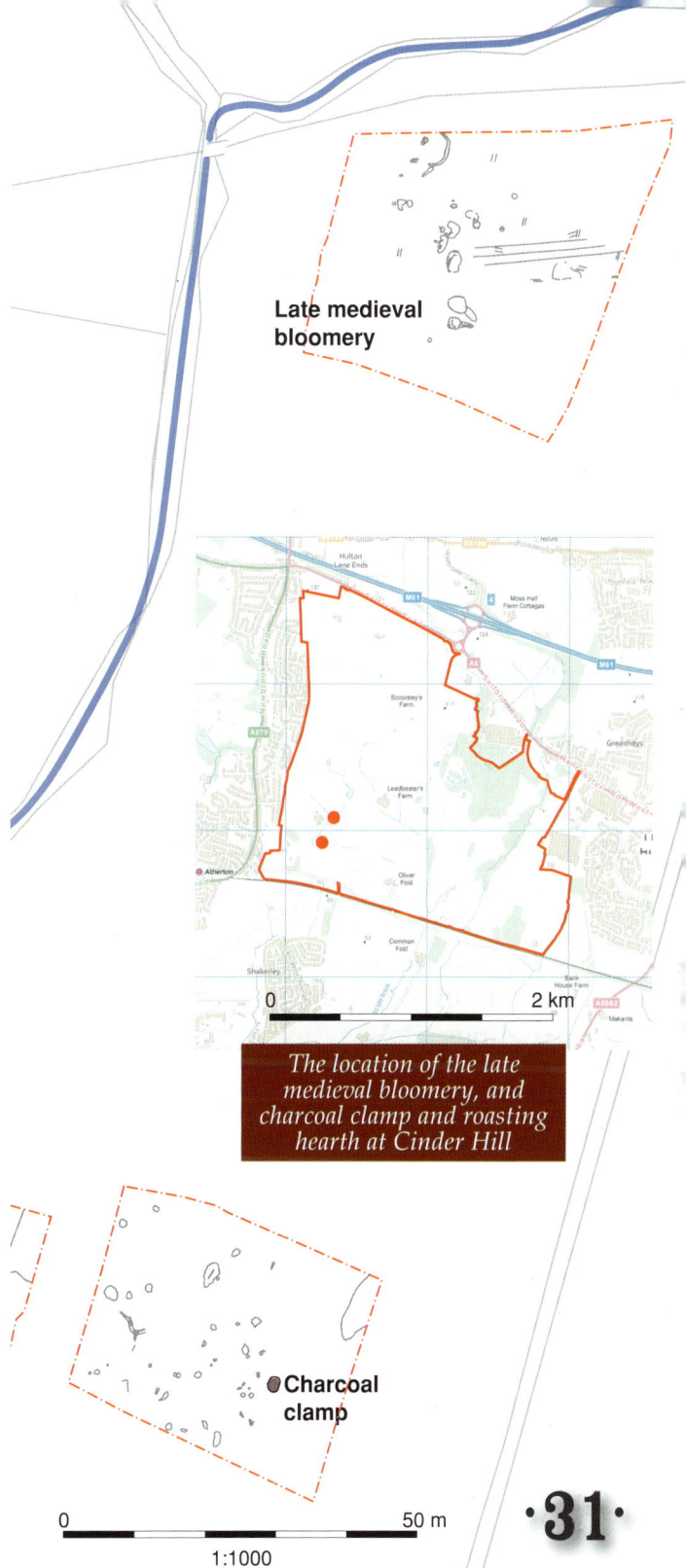

Late medieval bloomery

The location of the late medieval bloomery, and charcoal clamp and roasting hearth at Cinder Hill

0   2 km

Charcoal clamp

0   50 m

1:1000

The actual form of a typical late medieval bloomery consisted of small cylindrical furnaces, usually found in pairs. These had clay- and stone-lined bases, which formed a hearth, and upper walls built of wood and thick clay. These walls formed the body of the furnace and also acted as a chimney. To smelt iron ore, charcoal was placed inside the furnace and set alight. A pair of bellows, pumped by foot or hand, was then placed through a blowing hole, at the base of the hearth, to produce a continual supply of air that raised the temperature within the furnace. The fire was constantly fed with charcoal and air, and when the correct temperature was reached (c 1250°C) the ore would be placed through the open top of the furnace. When melted, the iron would run down into the hearth where it would pool, forming a bloom of wrought iron. Once the smelting process had begun, the impurities (the slag) would also leave through the furnace's mouth, or tapping arch, and would travel along a tapping channel, being then collected in a slag-tapping pit.

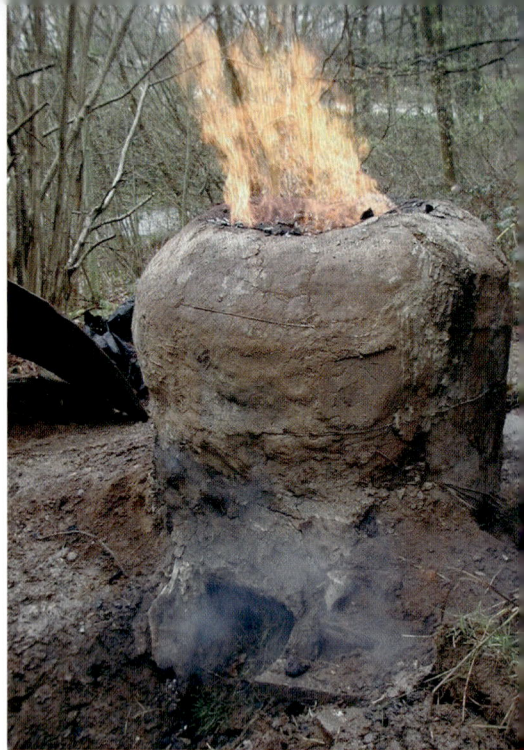

A reconstructed medieval furnace comparable to those found at Cinder Hill (Courtesy of Tim Young)

In addition to the furnace, a second hearth was sometimes close by, which is known as a stringhearth or reheating hearth. In this, the bloom was reheated and the remaining waste inclusions could be hammered out. Indeed, experiments into ancient iron-working techniques indicate that a cold 2kg bloom might require 20 to 25 heats before it could be brought up to the correct temperature for final consolidation into a billet.

Significantly, the remains present at Cinder Hill corresponded exactly to the typical layout of a medieval bloomery site, containing evidence for most of the processes connected with early iron production. For instance, the base of a charcoal clamp was discovered to the south of the bloomery, used to produce the charcoal fuel required by the iron-smelting process.

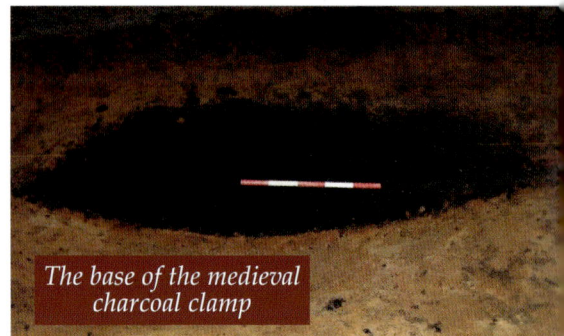

The base of the medieval charcoal clamp

This clamp would have been composed of wood, stacked in layers around a central vertical stake. The structure would then have been covered with earth and turf, and the central stake removed to form a flue. The clamp would be lit, by pouring burning coals down the flue, which lit the wood. The flue was then plugged and the stack would be left to smoulder for two days, to remove the moisture and volatile material from the wood and convert it to charcoal. Further insights into this clamp were also gained through analysis of the associated charcoal. This indicated that mature, slow-growing oak, at least 50 years in age, was the fuel used for charcoal production.

The age of the oak charcoal is significant, as it indicates that it was not derived from coppiced woodland, whereby trees were cut down, leaving a stump which would produce new shoots that would grow into straight poles that could be 'harvested' on a rolling cycle. This was slightly surprising, as in areas of known medieval iron production, such as the Lake District, the woodland was extensively coppiced to provide a constant supply of charcoal. Therefore, the lack of coppiced wood at Cinder Hill may suggest that there were no managed woodlands in the Cutacre area. Indeed, it may be that once iron production began, any nearby stands of mature woodland were completely eradicated to produce the required charcoal. Hence, any subsequent iron production would only be possible once the woodland cover had sufficiently regenerated and could supply adequate supplies for charcoal production.

The remains associated with the actual bloomery comprised five possible furnaces, within which the iron ore was smelted, to produce the wrought-iron blooms. It also seems that some of the furnaces were associated with timber structures, functioning as windbreaks or shelters. Chemical analysis of the slag waste from the site suggested that the iron ore used for smelting was Carboniferous claystone ironstones, extracted from the local geology, probably through the digging of small pits. It is also likely that lumps of ore were roasted, prior to smelting, to reduce their moisture and sulphur content, and also break them into managably sized lumps.

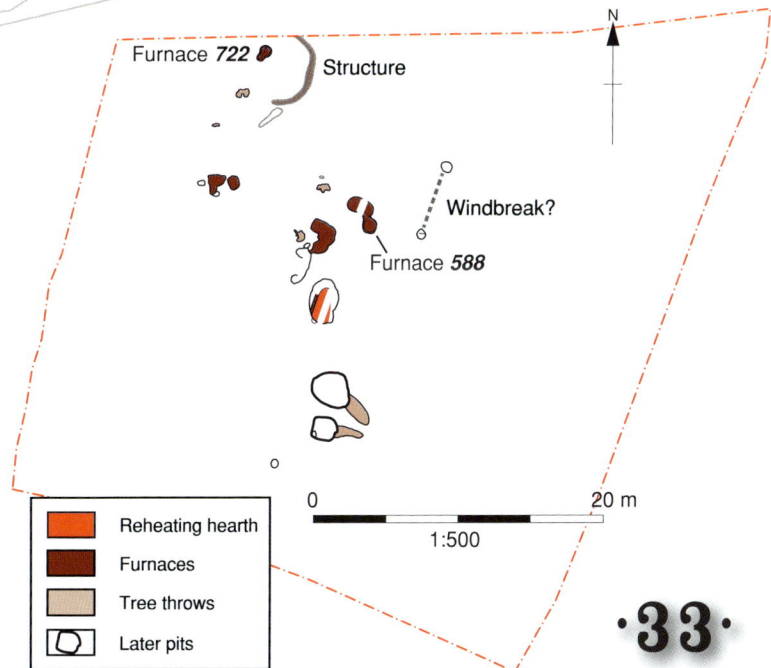

The late medieval bloomery at Cinder Hill

Furnace *722*

Structure

Windbreak?

Furnace *588*

N

0   20 m

1:500

Reheating hearth

Furnaces

Tree throws

Later pits

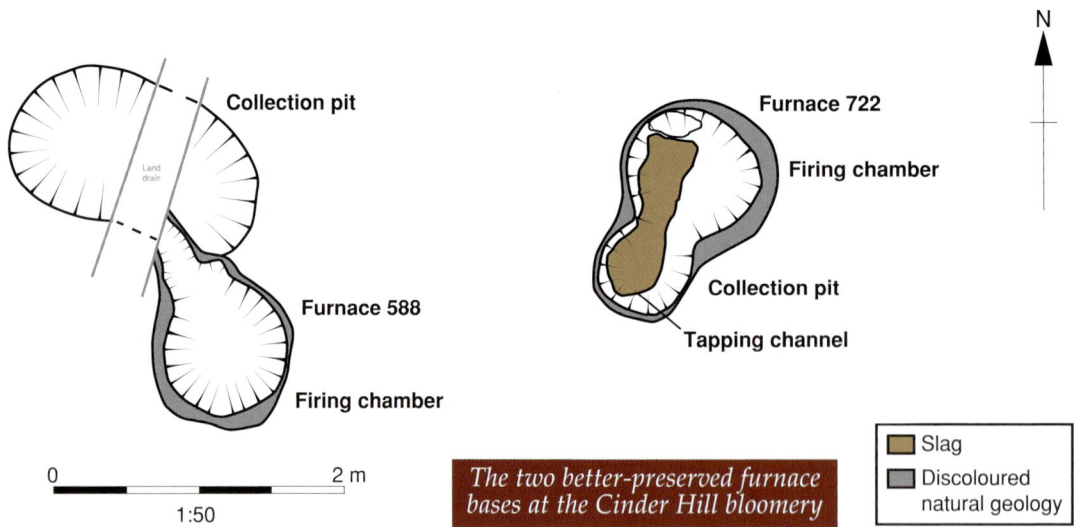

Collection pit

Land drain

Furnace 588

Firing chamber

Furnace 722

Firing chamber

Collection pit

Tapping channel

N

0   2 m

1:50

The two better-preserved furnace bases at the Cinder Hill bloomery

Slag

Discoloured natural geology

Only the bases of the furnaces survived, the two better-preserved of these, which were probably contemporary, both being defined by figure-of-eight-shaped shallow pits. In both cases, the respective pits contained the main circular firing chamber/hearth of the furnace, where the iron was smelted, the larger of which had a diameter of *c* 0.9m. Both the furnaces also had an opening, the tapping arch, which in turn was linked to a channel that fed into an adjacent pit. These were the tapping channel, and slag-tapping pit. Once the slag had cooled, it would then have been collected and dumped into spoil heaps, which probably littered the site.

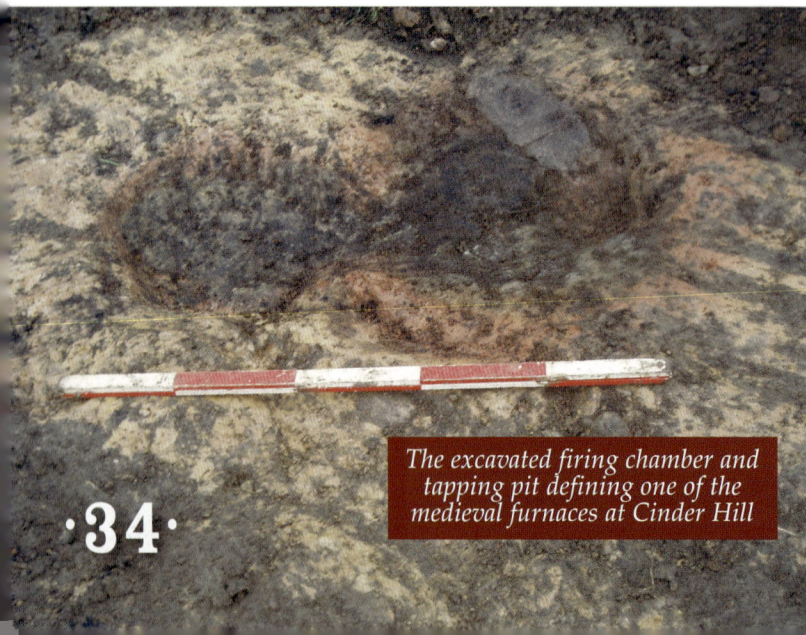

The excavated firing chamber and tapping pit defining one of the medieval furnaces at Cinder Hill

During the excavation, a total of 200kg of slag was collected, the majority of which was tapped bloomery iron-smelting slags. However, this quantity of material appears to represent only a small portion of the waste that may originally have been produced by the furnaces. It is estimated that it represents the residues from just 13 smelts although, in reality, each of the Cinder Hill furnaces would have been capable of being used for many tens of, and probably several hundred, smelts. Tellingly, a comparable medieval bloomery in the Castleshaw Valley produced an estimated 29 tonnes of slag, and it is probable that Cinder Hill originally contained an equivalent or greater amount, which has been removed from the site during later periods. Such 'waste' would have been rich in iron and may, therefore, have been converted into cast iron within a blast furnace, a more sophisticated form of iron-smelting furnace that was used in the North West from the late seventeenth century onwards.

A hearth was also identified in the medieval bloomery area at Cinder Hill that seems to be connected with the secondary processing of the iron blooms once they had been collected from the furnaces. Although this had been badly damaged by later activity, it was defined by a shallow scoop, surrounded by a halo of heat-affected natural clay. A fragment of slag was recovered from this area that, on analysis, was found to relate to the early stages of bloom compaction. Therefore, this seems to suggest that the hearth was used for reheating wrought-iron blooms, which could then be hammered into iron billets. Furthermore, one of these iron billets was discovered close to the hearth, and provides confirmation of the secondary processing of the iron blooms in this part of the site.

Several samples of charcoal obtained from the furnaces and other features at the site were radiocarbon dated, to determine the date of the bloomery. Whilst the dates indicate that iron production broadly occurred between the twelfth and fourteenth centuries, they also revealed that the site was used for iron production on at least three separate occasions. This suggests that the site was visited periodically to undertake smelting, probably by itinerant groups who

An example of an iron billet similar to that found at Cutacre

specialised in iron production, and who travelled quite widely. One further possibility, given the apparent absence of managed (coppiced) woodlands in the vicinity, is that these periodic episodes of iron production might directly relate to when adequate stands of woodland were available for charcoal production.

The Cinder Hill bloomery in context

The remains at Cinder Hill represent an excellent example of a late medieval bloomery, adding to the growing evidence for medieval iron production in Greater Manchester. To date, several sites have been subjected to excavation, but in contrast to Cinder Hill, Whitecarr Lane, Wythenshawe, Gadbury Fold, near Atherton, and Chorlton Fold, near

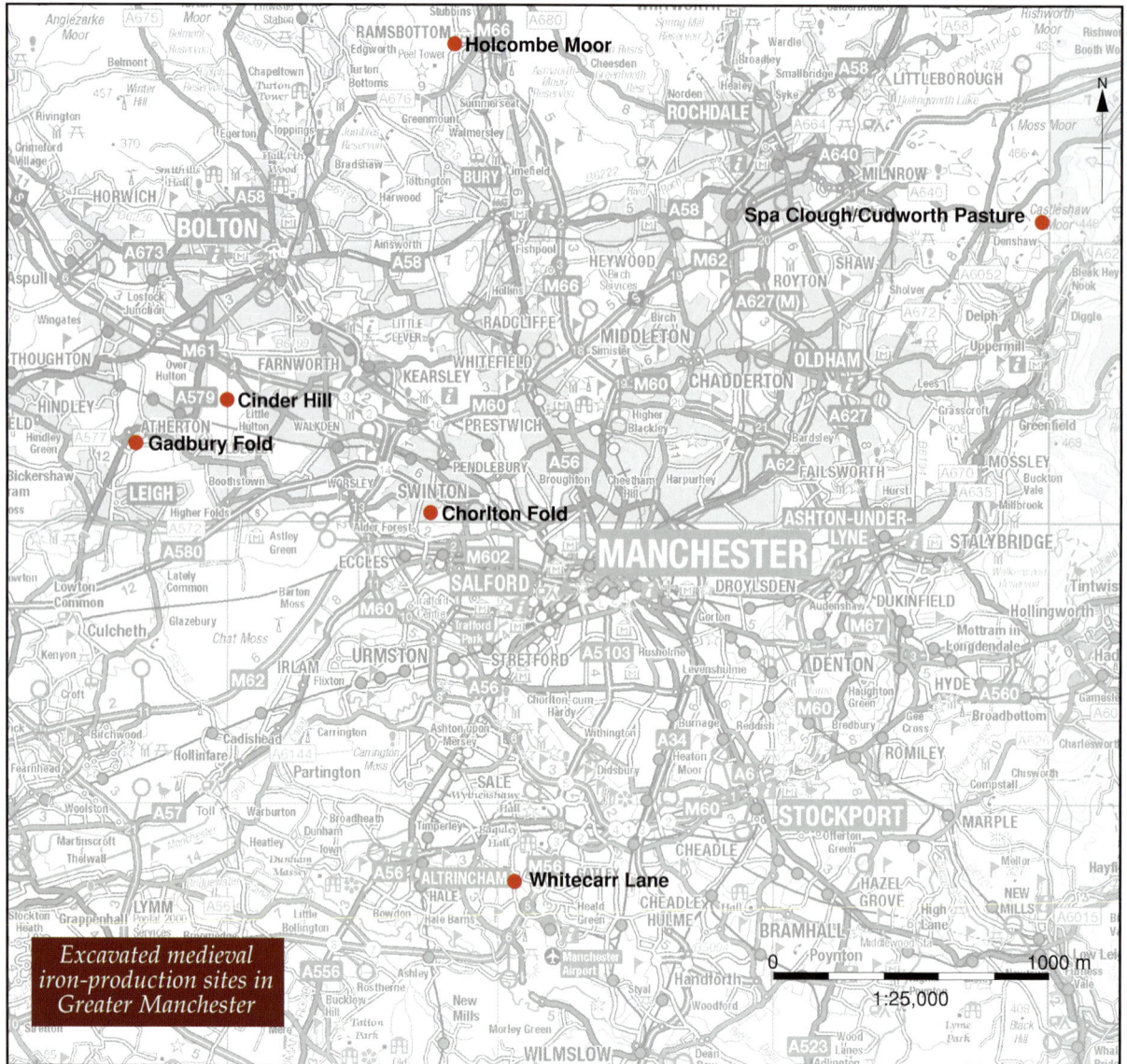

Excavated medieval iron-production sites in Greater Manchester

Monton, did not contain direct evidence for smelting furnaces. Instead, iron production is indicated by industrial residues and other associated features.

Two adjacent sites in the Castleshaw Valley have, however, produced more detailed evidence for late medieval iron production, largely comparable to that at Cinder Hill. These sites, known as Spa Clough and Cudworth Pasture, are some 200m apart and, as with Cinder Hill, they appear to contain the remains of iron production by itinerant smelters in the late medieval period, who exploited the local fuel and ore resources. At both sites, the bases of furnaces were excavated, of comparable design to the furnaces at Cinder Hill. Scientific dating places their use in the late twelfth/thirteenth century, the same general period as those from Cinder Hill. Other features at these sites were a revetment wall and post-pad, possibly supporting an awning, the remains of a possible charcoal clamp, an area where iron-ore was roasted, and a platform from which hot slag may have been raked to form a large spoil heap.

A furnace base, with tapping arch and channel, excavated at Spa Clough, Castleshaw (GMAAS archive)

In Greater Manchester, another site, on Holcombe Moor, has also revealed the remains of medieval iron production, at a place which also has the field-name 'Cinder Hill'. This site is the subject of ongoing excavation by the Holcombe Moor Heritage Group, which uncovered a well-preserved bloomery furnace in 2018. Although the furnace has been radiocarbon dated to cal AD 780-1020, fragments of pottery from the structure suggest that it more probably dates to the twelfth-fourteenth centuries.

A good portion of the archaeological remains recorded by the investigations at Cutacre dated to the post-medieval period, in the early seventeenth to late eighteenth centuries. This period is taken to begin at the time of the Dissolution of the Monasteries by Henry VIII in 1536-40, and in many parts of Greater Manchester continued up until the 1780s, when the Industrial Revolution really got underway.

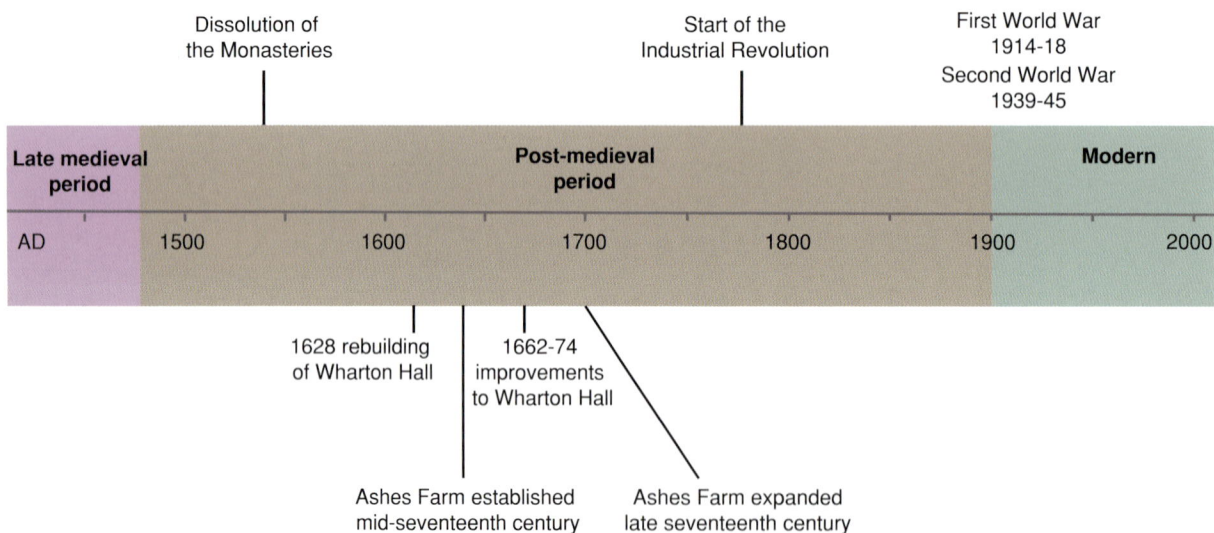

Dissolution of the Monasteries

Start of the Industrial Revolution

First World War 1914-18

Second World War 1939-45

Late medieval period	Post-medieval period	Modern

AD   1500   1600   1700   1800   1900   2000

1628 rebuilding of Wharton Hall

1662-74 improvements to Wharton Hall

Ashes Farm established mid-seventeenth century

Ashes Farm expanded late seventeenth century

Post-medieval settlements and rural industry

The main settlement in the eastern part of Cutacre, in Little Hulton township, was Wharton Hall. This was a high-status dwelling, whilst a nearby farm of lesser status, known as Hursts, after its early occupants, is also known. In addition, several post-medieval farms existed in the township of Tyldesley cum Shakerley, which can be traced back to the late sixteenth or seventeenth century, and within the Cutacre area these included Oliver Fold and Guest Fold.

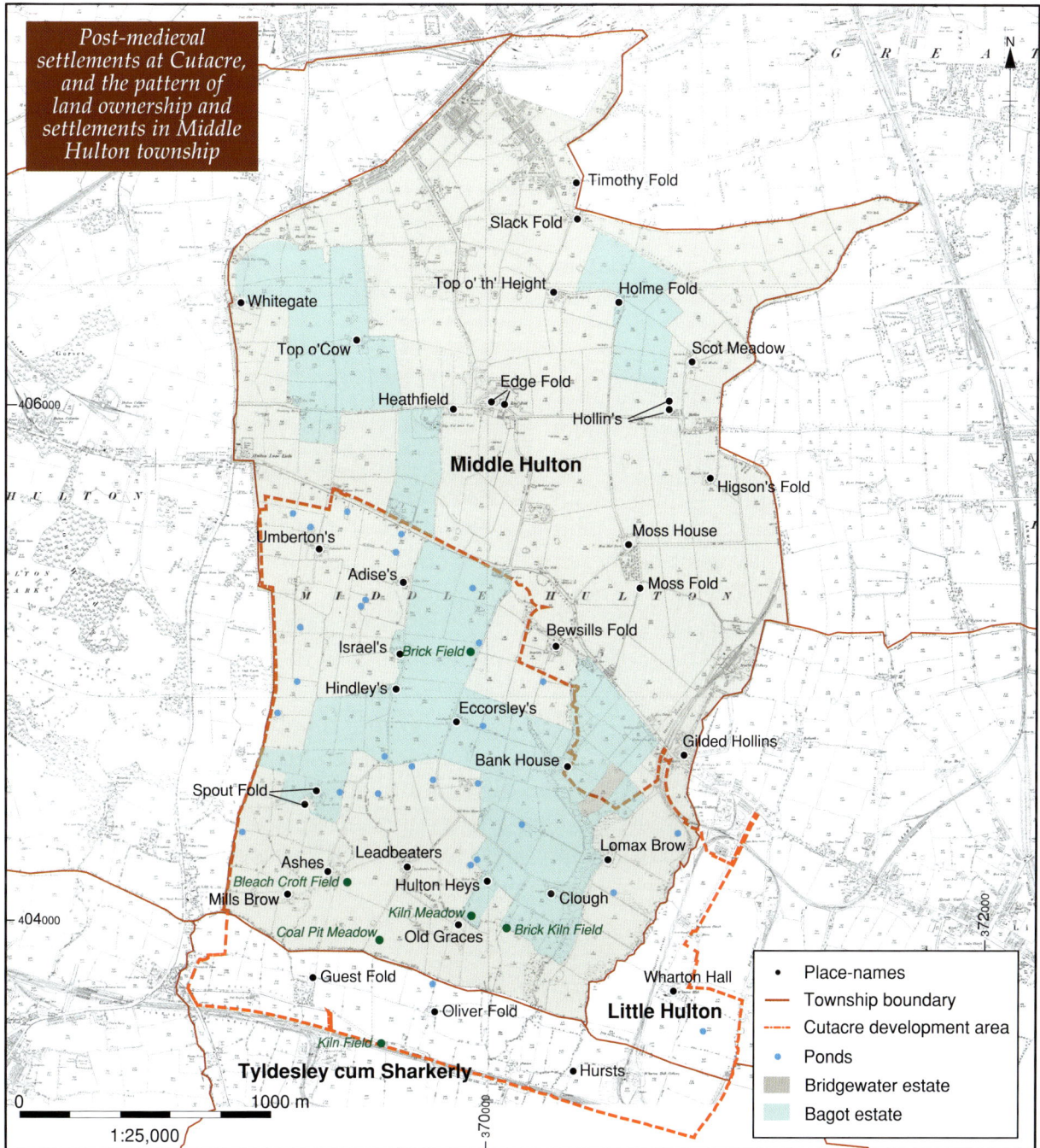

Post-medieval settlements at Cutacre, and the pattern of land ownership and settlements in Middle Hulton township

Timothy Fold
Slack Fold
Top o' th' Height
Holme Fold
Whitegate
Top o'Cow
Scot Meadow
Heathfield
Edge Fold
Hollin's
Middle Hulton
Higson's Fold
Umberton's
Moss House
Adise's
Moss Fold
M E D D L E   H U L T O N
Israel's   Brick Field
Bewsills Fold
Hindley's
Eccorsley's
Bank House
Gilded Hollins
Spout Fold
Lomax Brow
Ashes   Leadbeaters
Bleach Croft Field
Hulton Heys
Clough
Mills Brow
Kiln Meadow
Coal Pit Meadow   Old Graces   Brick Kiln Field
Guest Fold
Wharton Hall
Oliver Fold
Little Hulton
Kiln Field
Tyldesley cum Sharkerly
Hursts

Legend	
•	Place-names
—	Township boundary
–·–	Cutacre development area
•	Ponds
	Bridgewater estate
	Bagot estate

0   1000 m
1:25,000

·39·

The remaining parts of Cutacre were in Middle Hulton township. Therefore, much information about this area in the post-medieval period derives from the documents of the Egerton family (the Earls of Bridgewater, 1639-1803), who held this township in the seventeenth and eighteenth centuries. However, it is clear from the documentary evidence that in the early eighteenth century the Egertons' estate in Middle Hulton was partitioned, following the marriage of Honora Egerton to Thomas Arden Bagot, and hence after this time some areas were in the direct possession of the Bridgewater estate, whilst others formed part of the Bagot

An extract from the Bagot estate plan (dating to c 1772), showing one of the farms (Hulton Heys) in Middle Hulton (Courtesy of Manchester Libraries and Archives)

estate. Fortunately, estate plans exist, showing the areas of Middle Hulton held by both the Bagot and Bridgewater estates. These provide details of the farms and field-names. By examining these plans, along with other historical documents, it is possible to determine which farms were in existence by 1674. In addition, the historical estate plans also indicate that these farms continued to be occupied throughout much of the eighteenth century.

Although the inhabitants of the post-medieval farms were probably principally engaged in agriculture, there is evidence that other industries regularly supplemented some tenants' farming income. For instance, textile manufacture appears to have formed one of the principal cottage industries, as this is mentioned in late sixteenth- and early seventeenth-century probate records. Similarly, textile finishing, specifically involving the bleaching of cloth, is also recorded at Ashes farm in c 1764. The tenants at this farm also made a living as tanners.

Field-names, seen on historical maps, such as Brick Field, Brick Kiln Field, Kiln Meadow, and Kiln Field, suggest places where bricks were manufactured, probably on an *ad-hoc* basis to meet immediate local needs. These maps also depict numerous ponds in the Cutacre area. Some of these may have been dug to extract clay for brick making, whilst others might have been marl pits, from which calcareous clay was extracted to be spread as a fertiliser in neighbouring fields. Another post-medieval activity at Cutacre, evident from historical documents and maps, is coal mining. Specifically, the location of an early to mid-eighteenth-century mining site at the southern end of Middle Hulton township is indicated by the name of 'Coal Pit Meadow', whilst a lease of 1795 mentions an old sough (*ie* a tunnel for draining mine workings) at Bank House Farm.

Wharton Hall: a high-status settlement

An important element of the Cutacre project was large-scale excavation at Wharton Hall. This allowed the development of a high-status post-medieval dwelling to be examined, which, in this case, seems to have been founded in the medieval period. There are several surviving historical documents relating to this site dating from the sixteenth century onwards, which allow some 'flesh' to be placed on the archaeological evidence, principally providing details of those people who owned and occupied the post-medieval hall.

Although these sources are slightly confusing, particularly as many of the owners/occupiers had the same name, it is clear that, throughout most of the sixteenth century, the hall was in the possession of the Warton family, the medieval owners of the Wharton estate. However, in the 1590s, its then owner, William Warton, known as 'the traitor', was accused of high treason for supporting the Catholic Church, and his lands were seized by the Crown. Eventually, in September 1596, the property was transferred to Ralph Ashton (the fifth in a line of family members of that name), who held the manor of Great Lever, near Bolton. Then, shortly after, the property passed back into the hands of the Warton family, but in 1613 was sold to Ralph Ashton (the sixth), who leased it to William Warton, a namesake of William Warton 'the traitor', who owned the property in the 1590s.

In 1628, Ralph Ashton sold the Wharton Hall estate to the Mort family. Wharton Hall remained in the hands of the Morts until *c* 1870, though from 1734 it passed through the female line of the family. During the seventeenth century, the Mort family represented an emerging class of Lancashire landowners, who, unlike the traditional gentry, who inherited their positions and land-holdings, set about actively acquiring wealth, manorial rights, and social status. Thus, Wharton Hall and its estate were purchased by the Mort family as part of this process of acquisition. In fact, at this time, this was the second high-status hall in the area that had been acquired by the Morts, with the other, Dam House (or Astley Hall), being close to Cutacre, in Tyldesley. This property was largely rebuilt in the 1650s and these elements are still standing, with the property currently being protected as a Grade II* Listed Building. By the early 1630s, the Morts also owned several estates in south Lancashire and Cheshire, which included the manor of Astley.

The first post-medieval hall

The post-medieval remains uncovered by the excavation at Wharton Hall were extensive and included several *in-situ* stone walls, and a 'robber' trench, where a stone wall had been dug out and removed. Together these defined the outline of the post-medieval hall. Originally these walls formed a stone plinth, that would have supported the timber-framed superstructure for the hall. Based on analogy with other comparable early post-medieval buildings, the areas between the framing might originally have been of wattle and daub, which at a later date would have been replaced with brick.

Dam House, a post-medieval high-status hall, purchased and rebuilt by the Mort family in the seventeenth century (GMAAS archive)

It was clear from the position of the walls that in its earliest incarnation the post-medieval hall measured *c* 19m long, and comprised a central range (the hall), with projecting cross-wings at either end. The central range would have formed both a living room and the area where cooking was undertaken; a will dating to 1631 suggests that it had a chamber

Phase 1
Early seventeenth century

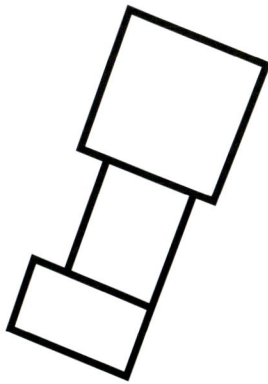

Phase 2
Late seventeenth century

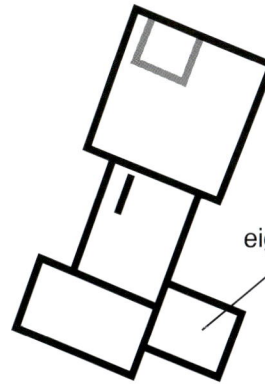

N

Refloored in
eighteenth century
(Phase 3)

0   10 m

1:200

The post-medieval development
of Wharton Hall

above that would have been a bedroom. Furthermore, based on the details contained in a lease of 1637, it is also possible that the northern cross-wing contained two parlours (used for seating and sleeping), described as the 'great parlour' and the 'litle parlour beneith the old wyves house', whilst the southern cross-wing contained two service rooms, named as 'the butterie and the storehouse'. Photographs of the hall taken during the late nineteenth and early twentieth centuries show that these cross-wings, like the central range, had two storeys, with upper bed chambers, and the southern cross-wing was jettied and coved at the first-floor level.

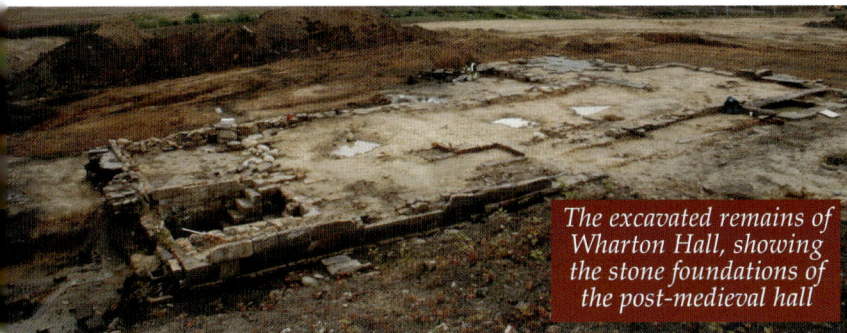

The excavated remains of Wharton Hall, showing the stone foundations of the post-medieval hall

Fortunately, during excavation of the post-medieval hall, it was clear that the foundations for its stone walls/plinth had been dug through a layer of soil which contained numerous fragments of datable pottery. It was evident from the dates of these objects that the building broadly dated to the late sixteenth or early part of the seventeenth century. Luckily, the dating of the building could be refined further, as it is known from nineteenth-century

An undated photograph of Wharton Hall, showing the jettied and coved southern cross-wing. The exterior of the post-medieval property had been refaced with brick, probably prior to the 1830s, and covered with a wash and painted in parts to resemble timber framing (from the Salford Local History Library Collection)

accounts that, when the hall was still standing, a timber beam was discovered that was inscribed with the date 1629. This date falls at the end of the date range provided by the pottery and was probably inscribed on the beam to commemorate the construction of this hall. Based on the known history of the property, it would have been built during the ownership of Adam Mort. In fact, Adam Mort acquired Wharton Hall in 1628, and it is therefore likely that he decided to demolish the existing and outdated medieval hall, and build a 'new', more 'modern' hall in its place.

This pattern of demolishing and rebuilding is not uncommon in Lancashire and Cheshire during the post-medieval period, and has also been recognised as a broader national trend, often referred to as the 'Great Rebuilding'. It seems to have been the outcome of rising levels of prosperity and also a desire to 'modernise' dwellings, introducing more comfortable designs, and Adam Mort, who throughout his life accrued various properties and land-holdings in the area, seems to have been actively engaged in this process.

One curious point is that, whilst Adam Mort seems to have invested in rebuilding this property, it is evident from the historical documents that he chose not to occupy the hall, but instead leased it out to tenants. Interestingly, the tenant who occupied the property at the time of Adam Mort's acquisition/rebuilding was William Warton, probably a descendant of the original medieval and sixteenth-century owners of the property. Of course, it is possible that, after rebuilding, Adam Mort did actually intend to move into Wharton Hall, but he died shortly after, in 1631. The property then passed to his son Thomas, who initially lived in his wife's family home at Smithfold, in Little Hulton, before acquiring Peel Hall, or Wicheves, also in Little Hulton, which became his principal residence. This site was also the subject of archaeological excavation in the late 1990s. However, whilst this work traced the course of the moat which had surrounded the early hall, it found only slight remains of what may have been the building within.

Late seventeenth-century and early eighteenth-century improvement

It was apparent from the archaeological remains that, following its construction in 1629, the post-medieval hall was improved and added to in the late seventeenth century. This most probably occurred between 1662 and 1664, when taxation documents (known as the Hearth Tax) indicate that the number of hearths in the property increased from four to seven, implying a phase of improvement and rebuilding. Given the known history of the property, this phase of rebuilding was the work of Robert Mort. He was the first of the family to occupy the house, from the early 1660s until 1692, and, given this, probably wished to improve it when he first became resident.

Under Robert Mort, Wharton Hall also became a place of worship for some Protestant religious groups (Non-Conformists/dissenters) that disagreed with the teachings and beliefs of the Church of England. The rise and influence of Non-Conformism is a characteristic feature of the late seventeenth

The Non-Conformist graveyard at Wharton Lane (Image Copyright Anthony Parkes. This work is licensed under the Creative Commons Attribution-Share Alike 2.0 Generic Licence)

century in Lancashire, and Non-Conformists continued to hold sway over local politics throughout the eighteenth and nineteenth centuries. Indeed, the use of Wharton Hall as a place for their worship continued into the early eighteenth century, when in 1709, Robert's son, Nathan Mort, obtained a licence for it to be a dissenters' meeting place, in this instance used for Presbyterian services. Slightly later, in 1723, a purpose-built Presbyterian chapel was constructed to the north of the hall, adjacent to Wharton Lane, though this was rebuilt in 1901. The chapel was demolished in the late twentieth century, but the graveyard remains.

A photograph of Wharton Hall dating to 1930, with the extended northern cross-wing on the left and the southern cross-wing on the right (courtesy of Manchester Libraries and Archives)

The archaeological evidence indicates that the late seventeenth-century improvements at Wharton Hall included the insertion of a fireplace with a stone stack into the central range. Other improvements were the rebuilding and extending of the northern cross-wing, as well as the construction of a small cellar within the extended area, that would have been used for storage. This phase of rebuilding added 3m onto the length of the hall, the remodelled northern cross-wing being visible on an early twentieth-century photograph. A small extension was also added onto the southern cross-wing, perhaps functioning as a kitchen. The insertion of a dedicated kitchen is important as it would have allowed cooking to be moved out of the main living room (the central range), creating a clearer definition of domestic space. This reflects a wider trend, as from the late seventeenth century onwards such dedicated rooms often became incorporated into the main block of a post-medieval hall. It was evident that the kitchen was also refloored in the eighteenth century, during a time when the hall was still owned by the Mort family (either directly, then through the female line), but was in the hands of tenants.

The cellar in the late seventeenth-century extension of Wharton Hall's northern cross-wing

Ashes farm: a lower-status settlement

Another important element of the Cutacre project was large-scale excavation at Ashes, one of the post-medieval farmsteads within Middle Hulton, on land owned by the Bridgewater estate. This was probably typical of the farmsteads that existed in the wider area during the seventeenth and eighteenth centuries. Again, as with Wharton Hall, excavation provided excellent insights into the development of this settlement, which was of a lesser status.

The excavated remains of Ashes, a post-medieval farmstead

Perhaps significantly, this farm was close to Cinder Hill and hence it is possible that its name 'Ashes' is another reference to the medieval bloomery site that was discovered and excavated there. Analysis of the documentary evidence allowed its post-medieval occupants to be discerned and also provided valuable details that could be combined with the archaeological evidence. Interestingly, the historical sources indicated that this farm was tenanted by members of the Mort family from the seventeenth century until the early nineteenth, and was often referred to as 'Mort Fold'. It therefore seems likely that the Mort family of Middle Hulton had a common ancestry with the Morts of Wharton Hall, but the precise relationship is not known.

An expanding seventeenth- and early eighteenth-century farm

The post-medieval remains encountered at Ashes were similar to those at Wharton Hall, in that they comprised stone and brick walls, and floors. It was evident from these, together with the documentary evidence, that the first farmhouse dated to the mid-seventeenth century, and its earliest occupant was Henry Mort. This house was defined by stone walls, which probably acted as a plinth for a timber-framed superstructure, and it had a rectangular plan.

Two-cell house, mid-seventeenth century

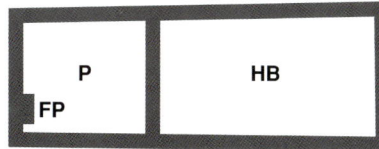

Double-depth house, late seventeenth century

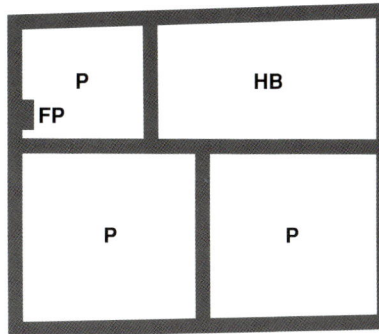

HB	Housebody
P	Parlour
FP	Fireplace

1:200

The seventeenth-century development of Ashes

The remains indicated that the house was initially of single depth (single-room deep), measuring 10.25 x 3.75m, and contained two rooms. This style of post-medieval rural house is described as a 'two-cell house', and it was a common type in rural Lancashire during the seventeenth century. In such houses, one room (usually the larger) formed the main housebody, which was the living room/kitchen and thus contained the principal fireplace, and the other was a parlour, more private space, also used for sleeping. Although many parlours within similar houses dating to this period were unheated, at Ashes the remains of a fireplace were evident. Many seventeenth-century two-cell houses also had a first floor that contained one or two bed chambers, and this was probably the case at Ashes, as documentary evidence dating to the late seventeenth century mentions a chamber over the parlour.

Another feature of the mid-seventeenth-century house was a substantial cellar. Originally, this formed a single basement room beneath the housebody, provided with a stone-mullioned window, giving some natural lighting. This cellar also contained a recessed stone-built cupboard, and was probably used to store food and also the products of any cottage industries that occurred at the farm.

At some stage in the late seventeenth century, the archaeology indicated that Ashes was substantially expanded in size. It is possible that this was undertaken by John Mort, the son of Henry Mort, Ashes' first occupant, who took over the lease of the property following his father's death in 1685. This expansion involved the construction of two additional rooms, with stone footings, that were attached to the southern side of the original two-cell house.

The eastern room at Ashes, which functioned as a parlour

These therefore transformed the building into a medium-sized house, which was two rooms deep, containing four compactly arranged ground-floor rooms. Fortunately, the documentary evidence provides further details of the internal arrangements. The will of John Mort, who died in 1691, mentions the housebody (referred to as 'the firehouse') and three parlours. This might suggest that the original mid-seventeenth-century housebody and parlour were retained, with two additional parlours. One curious feature with this arrangement is that the two additional rooms were larger in size than those associated with the original house. This might suggest that there was a more radical reorganisation of space within this late seventeenth-century farmhouse; indeed, one possible suggestion is that the main living/kitchen area was transferred from the original mid-seventeenth-century housebody into one of the new, larger 'parlour' rooms.

The plan of the late seventeenth-century house at Ashes is also significant in other ways, as it mimics a type of purpose-built rural farmhouse that became very widespread across Lancashire between the mid-eighteenth and late nineteenth centuries, although their origins were in the latter half of the seventeenth century. This is known as a 'double-pile' house. Although, in contrast to Ashes, most examples normally contain a central lobby entrance, or in some early examples a gable-end entrance, with pairs of rooms arranged on either side, it does seem possible that those who constructed the extensions at Ashes were inspired by this new style of house design.

The archaeological remains indicated that Ashes underwent a further stage of expansion in the earlier part of the eighteenth century, when the farm was leased by either Robert Mort, who died in 1728, or his son and successor John Mort, who was tenant until his death in 1784. This expansion entailed the construction of another large room, tagged onto the western side of the farmhouse, which created a house with an L-shaped ground plan.

The progressive expansion of Ashes suggests that the Mort family of Middle Hulton, who built, expanded and occupied this property throughout the post-medieval period, were comparatively wealthy. The documentary evidence indicates that the family's wealth was not solely generated by farming, but also by additional activities, which may in fact have generated higher sources of income. In the seventeenth century these comprised tanning, and by the mid-eighteenth century included bleaching, indicating a connection with the domestic textile industry of this area.

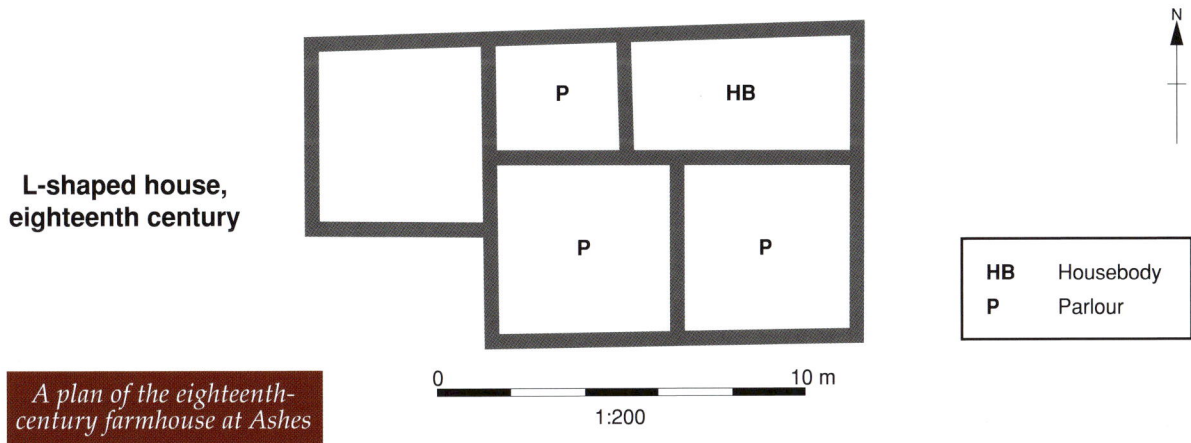

L-shaped house, eighteenth century

| HB | Housebody |
| P | Parlour |

0 _____ 10 m

1:200

A plan of the eighteenth-century farmhouse at Ashes

From the late eighteenth century onwards, south-east Lancashire, including the area now covered by Greater Manchester, was catapulted into the industrial era. This was characterised by the dramatic rise of the textile industry, particularly following the adoption of steam power, the appearance of industrial towns to house the ever-growing workforce, and a rise in coal mining, which procured the fuel needed to power this industrial age. Cutacre was greatly shaped by this latter industry and, by the 1840s, coal was being mined in a number of small collieries in the area. The scale of the industry increased in the late nineteenth century, when several large collieries were established. For instance, Wharton Hall Colliery, to the south of Wharton Hall, was established around 1870, whilst other large collieries just beyond the boundary of Cutacre included the Peel Hall Collieries to the east, and Charlton Colliery to the north. These were to have a dramatic effect on the local landscape, particularly in the vicinity of Wharton Hall, which was described by John Partington in the early twentieth century as being 'buried amidst coal-pit heaps'.

Although coal mining progressively dominated the Cutacre landscape, many of the post-medieval farmsteads, along with Wharton Hall, were still occupied and their tenants were actively engaged in farming. For example, at Ashes, following the death of John Mort in 1784, the farm passed into the hands of his son, Robert, who continued to occupy the farm until c 1802. After this time the tenancy passed to the Ashcroft family, who occupied the farm for over a century. During the excavation of the site, remains were identified that indicated that the farmhouse had been modified by either Robert Mort or the Ashcroft family. This modification involved rebuilding fairly large parts of the earlier post-medieval farmhouse in brick, probably to modernise what, by then, may have been a fairly dilapidated and outdated building. This 'modernisation' also involved remodelling the seventeenth-century cellar, by adding brick dividing walls, and brick-built fireplaces in some of the rooms within the farmhouse. Several small additional rooms were also added to the western end of the farmhouse, one of which contained a furnace, that was perhaps used in the smithing of agricultural tools.

The remodelled seventeenth-century cellar at Ashes, with later brick dividing walls

Similarly, excavation at Wharton Hall also identified remains which dated to the nineteenth century. The documentary evidence indicates that during this period the hall, as it had been in the earlier part of the eighteenth century, was occupied by various tenants, who, from *c* 1780 until the close of the nineteenth century, comprised successive generations of the Green family. The modifications undertaken to the hall during their residency included rebuilding and expanding the eastern end of the southern cross-wing in the early/mid-nineteenth century, which was then further modified in the late nineteenth century.

Late nineteenth-century collieries in the vicinity of Wharton Hall depicted on an Ordnance Survey map of 1891

The archaeological excavations at Cutacre were a great success and have clearly produced valuable evidence relevant to the development and use of a rural area that historically lay in south-east Lancashire. The evidence for prehistoric activity is particularly noteworthy, as this indicated that the landscape at Cutacre was utilised by the earliest communities within what is now Greater Manchester. Furthermore, this evidence can be compared directly with prehistoric remains known from

The remains of the southern cross-wing of Wharton Hall, with nineteenth-century additions

the Mersey Basin, and also from a wider area of north-west England. Indeed, some of the prehistoric remains from Cutacre, specifically those relating to the Middle Bronze Age settlement, hold great significance in that they are, to date, unique in Greater Manchester and, in terms of the wider prehistoric archaeology of the North West, they represent a rare example of settlement dating to this period.

Similarly, the evidence for medieval iron production is also extremely valuable. Although, in the North West, this industry was probably fairly commonplace, particularly in Cumbria, these types of site have only occasionally been examined archaeologically within Greater Manchester/south-east Lancashire. Therefore, the remains at Cutacre are extremely

Excavated medieval furnace base at Cinder Hill

significant in that they provide a rare example of an excavated medieval bloomery site, which, in turn, forms an important addition to the small regional corpus of comparable sites that currently exists.

Another major success of the project was the information it provided on post-medieval rural settlement. Indeed, through documentary research and open-area excavation, the project produced valuable data on two different classes of houses that existed within Greater Manchester. One of these, the farmhouse at Ashes, was seemingly occupied by a relatively wealthy family of tenant farmers, whilst the other was a more affluent form of rural house, typical of the halls which, at certain times, were home to the region's gentry. Significantly, the archaeological remains indicated that these houses were established and expanded in the seventeenth century and therefore provide excellent data on how certain early post-medieval house types developed over time.

ARCHAEOLOGY AND DEVELOPMENT

This booklet has described the archaeology of the area now forming the Cutacre Country Park. Significantly, the below-ground archaeology allows some insights into aspects of the early landscape, in particular, those existing in the prehistoric, medieval and post-medieval periods. In a similar way to many other developer-funded archaeological investigations, this work was devised through consultation with a regional archaeological curatorial body, which in this case was the Greater Manchester Archaeological Advisory Service (formerly the Greater Manchester Archaeological Unit). Its remit is to provide planning advice prior to any new development, which might have an impact on buried and/or upstanding remains. This advice is in accordance with national guidelines, specifically those covered by the National Planning Policy Framework, which was introduced in March 2012 (revised in 2019) as a means of conserving and enhancing the historic environment.

Surveying the archaeological remains at Ashes

If it is felt that the proposed development will have an impact on archaeological remains, the curatorial bodies will recommend that the developers fund a programme of archaeological investigation. Normally, a desk-based assessment forms the first phase of this investigation, which will be completed on behalf of the developer by an archaeological consultant, or contracting unit. Such assessments are designed to determine the presence and likely survival of any potential archaeological sites within the proposed development area. If, following assessment, it is felt that archaeological remains might be present, a phase of archaeological survey and excavation may be recommended, which again is funded by the developer.

Archaeological survey is used to record any visible remains, such as earthworks, or upstanding buildings. However, survey techniques also exist that can be used to detect below-ground remains that are not visible at surface level. These comprise geophysical survey, which in the case of Cutacre proved important for mapping the remains associated with the medieval iron bloomery.

Archaeological excavation will initially take the form of an evaluation, which is usually undertaken by an archaeological unit such as Oxford Archaeology North. This type of excavation normally involves trial trenching, which targets the areas of archaeological potential identified by the desk-based assessment and also by any archaeological surveys that have been completed on the site. The aim of this trenching is to determine the presence, or absence, of buried remains and, if present, to establish their date and state of preservation.

Depending on the results of this evaluation, a further phase of archaeological excavation may be recommended. This, often larger-scale, excavation focuses on the areas which have been identified by the evaluation as having archaeological significance. This excavation often exposes large open areas, to uncover the extent of any significant archaeological remains. During this phase of work, the archaeological structures and deposits are excavated and recorded, and all artefacts identified are collected.

After the archaeological fieldwork has been completed, the results from all phases of the work are outlined in a series of illustrated reports. Analysis and publication follows, together with compiling a project archive, deposited in the relevant local museum or other repository. These archives contain all the primary site records, photographs, and finds, and can be consulted by future researchers.

Recording the remains of Wharton Hall

·57·

GLOSSARY

BLOOMERY: charcoal-fired furnace for the direct reduction of iron ore to a bloom (a mass of iron and slag) of **wrought iron**.

CAL BC/CAL AD: **radiocarbon dates** that have been calibrated using tree-ring data.

COPPICING: traditional method of woodland management, which involves cutting back a tree or shrub to ground level to stimulate new growth from the stump/roots. After several years, the coppiced tree is harvested and the cycle begins again.

DOUBLE-PILE: a house that is two rooms deep and two rooms wide.

FINISHING: after cloth has been woven, it goes through a series of finishing processes, which can include bleaching, dyeing, and printing.

FOUR-POST STRUCTURE: a small prehistoric structure, with a raised floor, often interpreted as being for the storage or processing of grain.

GRISAILLE: a method of painting in grey monochrome, which was used on stained-glass windows.

HEARTH TAX: a tax that was levied on householders between 1662 and 1689. The tax records the name of the head of the household and the numbers of hearths/fires/stoves that were present at each property. Each household had to pay a shilling twice a year for each hearth in their property.

HER: Historic Environment Record; a database of information on archaeological sites, monuments, and buildings, which is maintained by a County or Unitary Authority.

HOUSEBODY: the main living room in a post-medieval house. The room contained the main heat source, which was also used for cooking.

MICROLITHS: small Mesolithic stone tools, usually with geometric and crescent forms. They were often hafted together to make composite tools.

MULLION: vertical upright dividing a window into lights.

PALAEOCHANNEL: a remnant of an inactive river or stream that has been infilled with sediment.

PARLOUR: a subsidiary room within a post-medieval house that was used for comfortable seating and sleeping.

RADIOCARBON DATING: a method of dating ancient organic material. It involves the measurement of the amounts of radiocarbon (which is subject to decay) remaining in organic matter.

ROUNDHOUSE: a circular or oval building that became the archetypal rural domestic dwelling throughout the second and first millennia BC, and also into the early Roman period. These houses ranged in size and could be constructed solely in timber, or have stone footings, which supported a timber superstructure.

STRINGHEARTH: a subsidiary hearth at an iron-production site used to reheat the iron bloom prior to hammering, to drive out slag and other impurities.

WROUGHT IRON: an iron alloy, with a very low carbon content and fibrous inclusions.

FURTHER READING

Bradley, R, 2007 *The Prehistory of Britain and Ireland*, Cambridge

Brennand, M (ed), 2006 *The Archaeology of North West England, Volume 1: Resource Assessment*, Archaeology North West, **8**, Manchester

Brunskill, R W, 1997 *Houses and Cottages of Britain: Origins and Development of Traditional Buildings*, London

Gregory, R A, Arrowsmith, P, Miller, I, Nevell, M, forthcoming *Farmers and Weavers: Archaeological Investigations at Kingsway Business Park and Cutacre Country Park, Greater Manchester*, Lancaster Imprints

Higham, N, 2004 *A Frontier Landscape: the North West in the Middle Ages*, Bollington

Kenyon, D, 1991 *The Origins of Lancashire*, Manchester

Paynter, S, 2011 *Introduction to Heritage Assets: Pre-industrial Ironworks*, London

Phillips, C B, and Smith, J H, 1994 *Lancashire and Cheshire from AD 1540*, London

Walton, J K, 1987 *Lancashire: a Social History 1558-1939*, Manchester

Copies of the detailed archaeological reports for this project have been deposited with the Greater Manchester Historic Environment Record, which is maintained by the Greater Manchester Archaeological Advisory Service (GMAAS)

Other pdf volumes in the Greater Manchester's Past Revealed *series can be downloaded at oxfordarchaeology.com/greatermanchesterspastrevealed, and diggreatermanchester.wordpress.com/publications*

Hard copies of some of these volumes are also available from GMAAS (email: gmaas@salford.ac.uk)